HITLER'S GERMANIC LEGIONS

LEGIONS

An illustrated history of
the Western European Legions
with the SS, 1941-1943

First published in 1978 by
Macdonald and Jane's Publishers Limited
Paulton House, 8 Shepherdess Walk,
London N1 7LW

ISBN 0 354 01110 3

Design: Judy Tuke

Printed in Great Britain by
Netherwood, Dalton and Co. Ltd.,
Huddersfield

HITLER'S GERMANIC
LEGIONS

An illustrated history of
the Western European Legions
with the SS, 1941–1943

Philip H Buss & Andrew Mollo

MACDONALD AND JANE'S · LONDON

The colour of the 1st Police Company of the Norwegian Legion is dipped in salute at a parade in Oslo to celebrate the unit's return from the eastern front; 6 April 1943

Contents

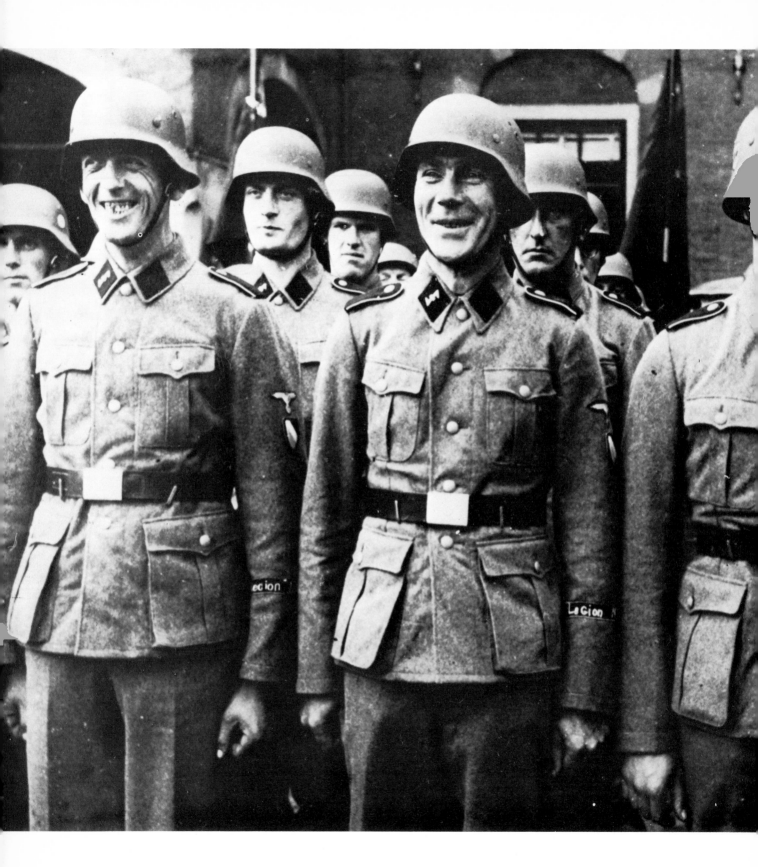

6

Preface

The long list of acknowledgements, which follows this preface, and the extensive bibliography at the end of this work may seem out of proportion to the extent and depth of this study, but it must be noted that this story of the Germanic legionary movement is a distillation of the researches of more than a quarter of a century. At one time I planned to use this material in a work dealing with the German Armed Forces in which I was to collaborate with the late Colonel Clifford M. Dodkins. His untimely death prevented this project from being completed, and I was therefore very pleased when Andrew Mollo suggested that we should work together on this volume.

Due in no small measure to the success of both wartime and post-war SS propaganda, and despite equally tendentious counter-propaganda, a legend has grown up which needs debunking. It is my great hope that nobody who reads this work will continue to be under the mistaken impression that the legions of the SS were either a dedicated force of anti-Communist crusaders or a band of ruthless and sadistic traitors.

There does not appear to have been an established sequence of seniority for the legions, but the order in which they are described here is consistent throughout, and is based on their date of formation and geographical grouping. Because the Finnish Battalion was not technically part of the Germanic legions, it has been included as an appendix. No attempt has been made to correct inaccuracies or inconsistencies in the original German documents quoted herein.

To differentiate between men who served with or in SS units without actually being members of the SS, it was decided to replace the 'SS' prefix by 'Legions'; thus an officer with the rank of *Untersturmführer* who was not an SS member was referred to as a *'Legions-Untersturmführer'*. This applied to all ranks usually up to *Standartenführer*. It would appear that on a day to day basis, however, the prefix 'SS' tended to be used, and the 'Legion' prefix appeared only on official correspondence, documents, and orders. To a great extent it depended on the attitude of the soldier concerned. If he was a pan-German he would try to use the SS prefix on every possible occasion, but if he was a nationalist (and sometimes even anti-SS) he would use the legionary one.

Acknowledgements

PHILIP BUSS

The material for this volume has accumulated over a number of years, in the course of which many individuals and institutions have provided valuable information.

Grateful acknowledgement is therefore made of the assistance, of the staffs of the Cabinet Office Historical Section, the Imperial War Museum, the Wiener Library, the Foreign Office Library and Records Department, and the Royal Institute of International Affairs. In addition, I remember with gratitude the help of the staffs of the Bundesarchiv in Koblenz, the Militärarchiv in Freiburg, and the Rijksinstituut voor Oorlogsdocumentatie in Amsterdam. I should also like to thank the custodians of the Legermuseum at Leiden, the Museet for Danmarks Frihedskamp in Copenhagen, the Musée Royal de l'Armée et d'Histoire Militaire, Brussels, and the Tøjhusmuseet in Copenhagen. I am also very grateful for the facilities provided by the libraries of the University of Kent at Canterbury, the City of Canterbury, the Borough of Redbridge, the University of Amsterdam, and the Canterbury College of Technology.

In addition to the staffs of the above institutions, I would also like to thank Thomas Claudius, the late Colonel C. M. Dodkins, Dr Martin Ellehauge, Hartvig Fleege, Dr Maurice Larkin, Dr Friedrich Herrmann, David Littlejohn, Warren Odegard, the late Friedhelm Ollenschläger, Major a.D. H. R. von Stein, Hugh Page Taylor, Dr Georg Tessin, and L. Westberg.

Finally, I must thank my wife and family for their forbearance during the years in which I have been engaged in collecting data for this and future volumes.

Philip H. Buss
Canterbury, April 1977

Leg. Sturmbannführer K. B. Martinsen as commander of the *'Freikorps Danmark'*. Martinsen went on to command the infamous Schalburg Corps, and after the war was executed for his involvement in a political murder

ANDREW MOLLO

My thanks are also due to all those listed above, but additionally I should like to mention those who, over the years, have supported my researches, and on whom I have come to rely for moral support (like my family), and for answers to my many questions: in particular, Mrs Johnson of the Wiener Library, Dr N. K. C. A. in't Veld of the Rijksinstituut voor Oorlogsdocumentatie in Amsterdam, Dr K. G. Klietmann, Hans van Brink, Ian Bogaert, Jan Poul Petersen, and Svante I: son Warfvinge. James van Fleet of Stanhope, New Jersey, and Per Mørk of Kongsberg, Norway, have kindly allowed me to photograph items of insignia from their collections. Bendt Nielsen has kindly made it possible for me to reproduce rare and hitherto unpublished photographs from the former DNSAP's Billedtjeneste. Brian L. Davis, W. Schneider, and Roy Smith have also provided rare photographic material, and Pierre Turner and Malcolm McGregor the drawings of colours. Nor do I forget the help provided by those who wish to remain anonymous.

Andrew Mollo
London, April 1977

Introduction

In the nineteenth and twentieth centuries it has become common practice to describe foreign contingents in national armies as legions. The choice of terminology is unfortunate, because foreign detachments have more in common with the *Auxilia* of ancient Rome, than with her *Legiones*.

During the middle ages it was not uncommon for a state to hire units of foreign mercenaries, such as the Genoese cross-bowmen or the Flemish hand-gunmen, for a specific campaign. Varangians and Scots were employed as royal bodyguards, and in the eighteenth century several European states employed foreign professionals from Switzerland, Germany, Scotland, and Ireland in permanent regiments. Today the only homogeneous units to survive are the Swiss Guard of the Vatican, and the Gurkhas.

At the beginning of the nineteenth century the term 'legion' came to be applied to detachments of émigré patriots seeking to free their country from foreign occupation; notable among these were Napoleon's Polish Lancers and the Hanoverian King's German Legion. During World War I, the term was also applied to units of Poles and Czechs seeking to attain national independence. During the Spanish Civil War, the International Brigades no longer fought for a country but for a political ideal.

Probably the most famous force of all is the French Foreign Legion, formed in the nineteenth century, and followed in this century by a Spanish Foreign Legion, which also still exists to this day. However, these legions form a permanent part of the armies of France and Spain and, unlike other foreign contingents, no attempt is made to segregate men by nationality.

The legions raised by the Waffen-SS during World War 2 had little in common with the Foreign Legions of France and Spain because the Germans attempted to organise ethnically homogeneous units. Nor were the German-raised legions intended as a permanent force, since they were formed for one purpose and one purpose only – the defeat of the Soviet Union. Had the war ended with German victory, the legions were to have been disbanded, their purpose having been served.

Since the war there has been a tendency to idealise and even romanticise the foreign contribution to the SS. A legend has arisen that the Germanic legions were a hand-picked body of magnificent specimens of Germanic manhood motivated by National Socialist ideals, and forged into an almost superhuman fighting force by the example and know-how of a hand-picked and dedicated team of SS instructors. It has even been suggested that the legionary movement against Communism was the precursor of the North Atlantic Treaty Organisation.

There is no doubt that, at the beginning, a genuine attempt was made to select only the very best of the volunteers who applied to join the legions; criminals and idlers were rejected, and adventurers discouraged from applying. At the beginning of the war, the majority of Waffen-SS men were still the arrogant standard-bearers of National Socialism, and they reacted violently to the many foreign volunteers who were neither Nazis nor even particularly pro-German, and who showed a complete lack of interest and even disrespect for SS ideals and aims. This attitude was particularly prevalent in the Danish *Freikorps*.

Unlike the great colonial powers, Germany had few military men with the experience and aptitude for dealing with foreigners. As soon as the volunteers arrived at German training centres they began to complain about the unfriendly and even brutal attitude of the 'Prussian' SS instructors. These SS men were sickened by the sight of the SS uniform being worn by nationals of recently defeated and 'dishonoured' nations, while below the surface was the inbred soldier's contempt for traitors. Despite SS efforts to eliminate criminals, some wormed their way into the legions and offended the mass of honest working-class volunteers. Corruption among the SS existed and this led to mutual contempt.

The average volunteer was working class, apolitical, and if anything a little immature. Typical was the twenty-year-old Dutchman Gerardus Mooyman, who became the first Germanic volunteer to win the coveted Knight's Cross of the Iron Cross. According to one of his comrades, Mooyman was not a particularly enthusiastic soldier, and on 13 February 1943 he was sulking in his dugout south of Lake Ilmen when the Soviets launched a tank attack on his position. Mooyman had almost to be dragged out by the ear by a German officer attached to the Dutch Legion. Mooyman then vented his fury on the Soviet tanks by knocking out thirteen of them before cooling off. Still alive today, he remembers with regret his youthful thirst for adventure, the sadness and shame of his devoutly Catholic family and friends when he donned the SS uniform, and the wasted years both during and after the war. Apart from the Knight's Cross, Mooyman's story is typical of a tragic generation which had not reached maturity when circumstances beyond its control obliged it to take sides. Having taken sides, those of this generation fought with varying degrees of courage in a terrible war and, like their victims, suffered untold hardships. But the greatest hardship of all was to return to one's country not as a hero but as a criminal.

Part I POLITICAL BAC

EUROPA IS AANGETREDEN!
MET DE ⚡⚡·STANDAARD WESTLAND IN DEN STRIJD
TEGEN HET BOLSJEWISME
AANMELDING: DEN HAAG, STADHOUDERSLAAN 132

A recruiting poster for SS Regiment *'Westland'* shows a European phalanx marching towards a fiendish Soviet soldier; July 1941

SS Manpower Problems

By the mid-1930s, Himmler's black-uniformed SS had outgrown its original task of acting as guards at political meetings. It had already undertaken such specialist tasks as the gathering of information relating to internal security, and providing guards for concentration camps. Himmler's dream of a 'state protection corps' consisting of SS, police, and concentration camp guards was beginning to materialise. But these developments – and much else that was happening in Hitler's Germany – were not viewed with much enthusiasm by the German Army, let alone by the police.

In the autumn of 1934 the German Ministry of Defence reluctantly agreed to the arming of certain SS units. These company-sized detachments began life on 24 September 1934 and were at first called 'Political Readiness Squads' (Politische Bereitschaften), and later SS-Verfügungstruppe or 'SS Special Disposal Troops'. As their names imply, their primary function was the protection of the National Socialist system, its government, and its leaders from the threat of a popular uprising, or a coup by the Armed Forces. But it was soon to demonstrate that its role was not purely passive, and as time went on the embryo Waffen-SS increasingly competed with the more conservative Army in training, tactics, and a thoroughly National Socialist esprit de corps. By the outbreak of World War 2, the armed SS had still not reached its statutory strength of a motorised infantry division.

At the beginning of the war, these armed units were frequently called the 'Bewaffnete-SS' (literally armed SS), but in late 1939 the term 'Waffen-SS' began to appear on official documents, and it was under this name, rather than any other, that the militarised SS, its command structure, administrative service, and schools became known throughout the world. On 22 April 1941 the term SS-Verfügungstruppe was officially abolished.

Although the SS-Verfügungstruppe was primarily an armed force at Hitler's disposal for the maintenance of order inside Germany, he also decreed that in time of war it was to serve at the front under Army command. Hitler believed that front-line experience was essential if such a force was to command the respect of the German people. He also insisted that the human material was to be of the highest calibre, and so restricted the size of the armed SS to between five and ten per cent of the peacetime strength of the Army.

On 1 December 1939 Himmler established an SS Recruiting Office (Ergänzungsamt der Waffen-SS*) within the SS-Hauptamt. Gottlob Berger – a cunning and able Swabian – was entrusted with the running of this office. His task was not easy because he had to find recruits in spite of the passive resistance of the Armed Forces, who were suspicious of all paramilitary forces outside their control and unwilling to relinquish the cream of German manhood to the SS.

By 1940 the SS was having difficulties in meeting its target from among those too young and too old to be eligible for military service in the Armed Forces. However, Himmler also held the post of Reichskommissar für die Festigung deutscher Volkstums (Reich Commissar for the Strengthening of German-dom – a sort of liaison office for Germans living abroad), and Berger availed himself of his master's contacts outside the Reich to circumvent Armed Forces' restrictions by recruiting abroad. Not only were non-Germans of Nordic blood and ethnic-Germans living abroad allowed to become members of the SS, but they were also exempt from conscription in the German Armed Forces.

Despite the fact that overt recruitment outside Germany was out of the question, and no pressure could be exerted in those territories where no German troops were present, more than one hundred foreigners were serving with the armed SS in May 1940. The largest contingent consisted of forty-two Swiss. The German victories of 1940 opened up a vast recruiting ground over which the Wehrmacht had no jurisdiction.

Following the defeat of France in the summer of 1940, German ground forces were reduced considerably, while the SS lost three Totenkopf-Standarten. However, shortly afterwards it was decided to increase the Army by doubling the number of its armoured divisions and by more than doubling the number of its motorised divisions, and this reorganisation also affected the armed SS. Hitler's insistence that the armed SS should remain a small, exclusive police force limited its expansion, but he allowed his own personal bodyguard to be increased from a regiment to a brigade, and agreed to the formation of a new SS division, on condition that it was recruited mainly from foreigners. For this expansion the SS was to receive only three per cent of the newly enlisted age groups, which meant that it had to fall back on foreign manpower. German casualties during the Polish and French campaigns had been moderate and the SS had been able to make good its losses from its share of the available German manpower, but when it began to look as if the war would last longer than expected, the SS had to cast its net further afield for its replacements.

*First official use of the term Waffen-SS.

SS-Gruppenführer und Generalleutnant der Waffen-SS Gottlob Berger

In July 1940 Hitler announced his decision to invade the Soviet Union, and in the same month directives were issued and planning began. Himmler was one of the first to know, and he wasted no time in informing Berger, who drew up his forecast of the SS manpower needs on 7 August 1940. From the beginning of the war, German recruits had been apportioned on the basis of sixty-six per cent to the Army, nine per cent to the Navy, and twenty-five per cent to the Luftwaffe. Those for the armed SS were subtracted from the Army's percentage on a quota established by Hitler himself. However, in August 1940, there was still a strong possibility that England would be invaded, and the Navy and Luftwaffe were demanding an increase of their percentages to forty and ten per cent respectively. Berger assumed that the SS would receive only two per cent, or 12,000 men, whereas he estimated that 18,000 recruits per year would be required. Consequently, he recommended that recruiting should start in earnest in the Germanic areas of western Europe and from among the ethnic-German populations *(Volksgruppen)* of south-eastern Europe. Berger did not anticipate any objections, provided the SS-recruited personnel were not available to the Wehrmacht. Finally, he requested permission to establish a recruiting office to deal with foreign countries.

Berger's recruiting staff had sufficient return for its efforts in western Europe to form two new regiments, *'Nordland'* and *'Westland'*, and to make the new division – at first called *'Germania'* and then *'Wiking'* – a feasible proposition. Nevertheless, even though an existing SS regiment *'Germania'* was transferred to the new formation, and other Reich Germans provided cadres, there were still large gaps in its ranks, when the first enthusiastic rush of National Socialist and pro-German volunteers had been signed-up, and recruiting figures began to drop. To fill the gaps, Berger drafted in Reich Germans and ethnic-Germans *(Volksdeutsche)* to such an extent that, when Germany invaded the Soviet Union, Division *'Wiking'* contained a mere 1,142 Germanic volunteers – 630 Dutchmen, 294 Norwegians, 216 Danes, 1 Swede, and 1 Swiss.

When news of the German attack on the Soviet Union reached the rest of Europe, German diplomatic agencies received offers of assistance from individuals resident in occupied countries, as well as in the Independent State of Croatia, and in neutral Spain and Portugal. Norwegians and Swedes were willing to enlist in Finnish in preference to German forces. The German government decided to accept these offers of assistance and to establish closed contingents of foreign nationals. A Spanish formation was established on 25 June, and almost simultaneously Danish and Norwegian units were called into existence. On 29 June 1941 Hitler gave his approval to the establishment of legions from foreigners who wished to participate in the war against the Soviet Union. It was determined that legions from the Germanic countries were to be the responsibility of the Waffen-SS, while those from the non-Germanic countries were to be organised by the German Army.

In order to settle the details relating to the new units, the German Foreign Office convened a meeting of interested parties on 30 June 1941. Apart from the Foreign Office, also represented at this meeting were the Foreign Section of the *Oberkommando der Wehrmacht,* the *SS-Führungshauptamt,* the German Plenipotentiary in Copenhagen, and the Foreign Section *(Auslandsorganisation)* of the NSDAP. It was agreed that non-German volunteers were to fight in German uniform because of international law, but they would wear national badges. They were to receive the same pay and allowances as the German serviceman, and those with previous military experience would hold a rank equivalent to their former one. It was not envisaged that volunteers should receive German citizenship. Those foreigners already serving in the Waffen-SS had signed on for two

Recruiting office for Regiment *'Nordland'* in Copenhagen. Sentries were provided by the Danish Storm Troops (Storm Afdeling); June 1941

years, the duration of the war, or for an agreed period, but the Wehrmacht had not yet decided on the length of engagement for its volunteers. The meeting considered how the volunteers were to be organised, and it was laid down that volunteers were to serve only in closed units – some of which were already in existence. The Waffen-SS, being responsible for volunteers from Germanic countries, had set up a *Freikorps** in Denmark and a *Freiwilligenverband* in Norway – both independent of Regiment *'Nordland'* – and a separate *Freiwilligenkorps* for the Netherlands and the Flemish parts of Belgium in addition to, and independent of, Regiment *'Westland'*.

The Wehrmacht was responsible for the large volunteer formation that was being created by the Spanish Armed Forces and the Falangist Party. Spaniards were to serve in all three branches of the Wehrmacht, but there was to be no separate Falangist formation. A Croatian volunteer formation was to be set up under the auspices of the Wehrmacht, whose High Command wanted Croats to serve in all three branches.

The delegates considered that few volunteers could be expected from other European countries. Finns, while already serving in Regiment *'Nordland'*, could hardly be expected to volunteer for the German Army when Finland was already fighting the Soviet Union. It was anticipated that the Swedes would probably prefer to volunteer for the Finnish armed forces. However, if enough came forward, a Swedish Volunteer Corps could be formed under the auspices of the SS. If the Finnish Army

---

* It has been suggested that the Danish contingent was called a *Freikorps* (and not a 'Legion') to commemorate an earlier Danish unit that had fought against the Bolsheviks at the end of the World War I, but research has revealed that there was no such unit. Dr Kurt Klietmann says that *'Freikorps'* was Kryssing's suggestion, in recognition of the German struggle against Bolshevism in the 1920s, but that later both Kryssing and the Germans found this designation restricting and even sycophantic.

was unable to cope with the equipping and training of Swedish volunteers, they were to be directed to German reception centres. It was also considered probable that a number of Danes would prefer the Finnish forces. Swiss volunteers were to be accepted, but it was agreed not to approach the Swiss government or launch an appeal for Swiss recruits. In fact, some Swiss were already serving in the Waffen-SS. Few volunteers were expected from Portugal, but if enough presented themselves it might be possible to incorporate them in the Spanish formation. No Portuguese legion was in fact formed. The conference reached no decisions about whether Walloons and the Frenchmen were to be accepted.

In some cases the Germans opposed enlistment. In spite of offers from inhabitants of the Protectorate of Bohemia and Moravia, Czechs were not to be accepted. Russian émigrés had expressed a willingness to serve with the Germans, but they were to be refused in a courteous fashion. An ostensible reason was that they ran too great a risk if captured by the Soviets. However, some White Russians served as interpreters, and others served in both the Danish *Freikorps* and the French Volunteer Legion. Inhabitants of the newly occupied Baltic areas were to be dealt with by the local German Military Commander, while Balts in Germany who presented themselves were to be dealt with in a dilatory fashion.

The non-German legions authorised by Hitler did not represent an important increase in the size of the German Army, but for the Waffen-SS they provided a considerable accession of strength. The SS could have had a far larger share of western European manpower, but Himmler was interested only in raising legions of Danes, Norwegians, Dutchmen, and Flemings, and although in need of additional manpower, it relinquished the Walloon Legion that it had sponsored to the Army because Himmler maintained that Walloons were not Germanic and that their presence in the SS might offend the Flemings. Even if it had wanted to, the SS would have had difficulty in providing cadres and facilities for a division of Spaniards, a regiment each of Frenchmen and Croats, and a battalion of Walloons, in addition to those already employed. Furthermore, in the summer of 1941 a long campaign against the Soviet Union was not anticipated, and Himmler probably thought that it was just not worthwhile compromising the racial purity of the SS for the sake of short-lived units that might never see action.

Small as they were, the legions had considerable propaganda value. Finland, Romania, Hungary, Slovakia, and Italy were allied with Germany. The presence of western Europeans and Croats in the ranks of the German forces gave Germany's act of aggression the semblance of a European crusade against Bolshevism. Not for nothing was Hitler's invasion compared with that of Napoleon, when in 1812 the Russian people spoke of the 'invasion by twelve languages'.

A contingent of Dutch volunteers is sworn-in at a ceremony in The Hague; 7 August 1941

Terms of service and material inducements

Before the war, volunteers for the *SS-Verfügungstruppe* signed on for an initial period of four years, and came for the most part from the ranks of the Hitler Youth via the *Allgemeine-SS*. Apart from meeting the strict racial standards of the SS, they had to be perfect physical specimens, and in this respect Heinrich Himmler was as fastidious as Frederick William of Prussia had been in the matter of the height of his Grenadiers. It was not, however, necessary for SS men to be of German origin, provided that they were of Nordic blood, and in 1938 Himmler authorised the enlistment of *Germanen* into the *SS-Verfügungstruppe*; by the end of that year twenty foreign volunteers had been accepted. In April and May 1940, shortly after the victory in the west, two new *SS-Verfügungstruppe* regiments were formed: the Danish-Norwegian Regiment 'Nordland', and the Dutch-Flemish Regiment 'Westland'. Himmler was so enthusiastic about these new additions to his army that he declared in September 1940, 'we must attract all the Nordic blood in the world to us, and so deprive our enemies of it, in order that never again will Nordic or Germanic blood fight against us'.

Danish volunteers wait to sign up with the SS Regiment 'Nordland'

They then have to strip and wait for the medical examination

SS-Brigadeführer Rediess, Senior SS and Police Commander in Norway, at a recruiting ceremony for Regiment 'Nordland'; Oslo, February 1941

Conditions of acceptance for foreign volunteers for the Germanic legions were less stringent than those for the Waffen-SS. Volunteers still had to be between seventeen and forty years old, but in the case of former officers and NCOs the upper age limit was raised. The minimum height was reduced to 1.65 m, and then later disregarded. Candidates had to be able to prove Aryan descent for two generations and to possess an upright character. Those accepted into the legions were not members of the Waffen-SS but of units attached to it. They received the same pay and allowances as members of the Waffen-SS, and were subject to the same penal code. They wore the uniform of the Waffen-SS but with additional national insignia, and generally speaking the conditions appeared attractive to those who were nationalist without being National Socialist, and anti-Communist without being anti-British or even pro-German.

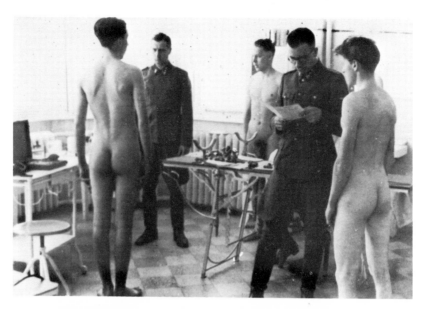

Germanic volunteers undergo a medical inspection

Arrival of a draft of volunteers for SS Regiment 'Westland' at the Freimann barracks, Munich; spring 1941

The material inducements for joining the legions were less than those of the Waffen-SS, for the simple reason that the legions were a temporary creation in which a volunteer was not expected to make his career. In the Waffen-SS, one could enlist for as long as twelve years and become eligible for German citizenship; like their German comrades, foreigners could on retirement take up a career in the German police or civil service, or receive land in the Incorporated Territories (Western Poland). In many cases, the legionaries were not affected by these advantages, because they left businesses and careers behind them at home. Pay was also less than they could earn in their homeland, but most volunteers probably anticipated a brief and victorious campaign, after which they would return home in triumph to privileged positions and the other advantages due to those who had thrown in their lot with the Germans.

Flemish volunteers in 'Westland' at rifle practice at Klagenfurt; May 1942

The contribution of political parties to the Legions

The contribution of National Socialist parties in occupied countries was not governed by the simple choice of whether to collaborate with the Germans or not. The questions were far more complex and were based to a large extent on the geo-political history of the country involved. First of all, it is necessary to identify German and SS aims, for the two were not always identical. Hitler's dream was the reconstitution of the Holy Roman Empire of the German people in its fullest geographical extent. He wanted to restore not merely the 1914 frontiers of the Second Reich, but repossess all the lands to which he thought Germany was entitled. The Netherlands and Flanders clearly qualified by virtue of their mediaeval status, but more practically Hitler wanted to control the mouths of the rivers Rhine, Meuse, and Scheldt.

Himmler was primarily interested in using the cream of Germanic blood to improve the racial composition of the German nation. Like Hitler, he also wanted to see the establishment of a National Socialist Greater German Reich, the cornerstone of which was to be one pan-Germanic SS organisation with branches in each of the newly incorporated territories. To this end the SS had by September 1940 already established a replica of the German *Allgemeine-SS* in Holland and Flanders; Norway followed in May 1941, and Denmark in February 1943. In April and May 1940, the Waffen-SS began to recruit foreign volunteers for the two new infantry regiments, '*Nordland*' and '*Westland*'. As chief SS recruiter, Berger's problem was that, although he knew of Hitler's plan to invade the Soviet Union in advance, he could not yet summon a crusade against Communism. All he could offer the citizens of countries recently defeated by Germany was the opportunity to become mercenaries in a crack German formation, and participate in a nebulous 'European war of liberation'. Surprisingly enough, this formula met with considerable initial success, but once all the enthusiastic Nazis and Germanophiles had been enrolled, recruiting began to dry up. Once the foreigners were in the SS, it was intended to indoctrinate them with SS values and aims so that when they returned home they would actively further the cause of National Socialism by joining the political wing of the SS in their homeland – the so-called *Germanische-SS*.

This was fine as far as the SS was concerned, but the right-wing nationalist and National Socialist parties were beginning to get the drift of German intentions. And because few of them wanted to be part of a unified pan-Germanic Reich, preferring instead autonomy within a federated National Socialist State, they decided, as a counter-weight to the expansion of the *Germanische-SS,* to put all their resources behind the legions.

Once the decision to form foreign volunteer legions had been taken, the rationale of the regiments 'Nordland', 'Westland' and 'Nordwest' became obsolete. The politically motivated volunteers were already serving with the above units, while only the keenest advocates of a Low German *(Dietse)* state would insist on joining 'Nordwest', with its Dutch and Flemish battalions. This left a vacuum which the political parties felt they could fill to their advantage.

In Holland, the situation was complicated by the existence of a number of small Fascist, Nazi, and pro-German or Nationalist parties. Even in the Dutch NSB *(National Socialistische Beweg-*

A recruiting pamphlet issued by the SS Recruiting Command in the Netherlands

ing) there were those, like Mussert himself, who did not want to see the Netherlands absorbed by Germany; others, so called annexationists, favoured union with the Reich. Mussert and the leader of the Flemish VNV *(Vlaamsche National Verbond)* Staf de Clercq, held similar views, but as a Dutch-Flemish state on a parity with Germany did not feature in German plans, the Germans were careful to prevent meetings between the two leaders, and saw to it that Dutch and Flemish units never served together. Mussert encouraged and later ordered his members to join the Dutch Legion in the hope that he would gain effective control over its employment. The Germans were aware that systematic infiltration could turn the legions into a sort of party militia or, even worse, into a new national army, and they watched the development of the legions carefully. Mussert's demand in March 1942 that the Legion return to the Netherlands to combat the resistance, and his hare-brained scheme in April to use the Dutch Legion to conquer South Africa were examples of this trend. Even so Mussert was still able to wring concessions from the Germans by threatening to withdraw his support for the recruitment of volunteers.

A month after he had taken a personal oath of loyalty to Adolf Hitler, Anton Mussert visited Dutchmen serving with Regiment 'Westland'. While in Munich he was also shown the main administrative building of the NSDAP. (l-r): *Reich* Commissar Seyss-Inquart, Mussert, Finance Minister Schwarz, and *Reichsführer-SS* Heinrich Himmler

Anton Mussert and *SS-Gruppenführer und Generalleutnant der Polizei* Hanns Rauter, the Senior SS and Police Commander in the Netherlands, July 1941

The leader of the Flemish National Association, VNV, laid down the terms which had to be met before he would cooperate in the raising of the Flemish Legion. First he demanded that the Flemish SS *(Vlaamsche-SS)* should stop poaching members of his party's para-military formation, the *Dietse Militie—Zwarte Brigade*. He insisted that he should handle the recruiting of members of the DMZB for 'Nordwest' and later for the Flemish Legion because he didn't want his supporters lost to the cause of Flemish nationalism in the Waffen-SS. His position in Flanders was sufficiently strong for Berger to concede to his demands, and this led to a large number of members of the DMZB, VNV, and other nationalist groups in the Legion.

Although some of the volunteers for the legions were undoubtedly anti-Communist before they enrolled – having been members of both separatist and annexationist right-wing parties – it would be wrong to suppose that they represented a majority. Dr Knoebel, in his work on the activities of the SS in Belgium, gives the party affiliations of the Flemings who had been accepted for the Waffen-SS and *Legion Flandern* by the summer of 1943.

Political Affiliation	Waffen-SS		Leg. Fland.		Overall	
	Total	%	Total	%	Total	%
Allgemeine-Germanische-SS (i.e. Algemeene Schutsscharen Vlaanderen)	202	13.32	246	9.35	448	10.80
Devlag (Deutsch-Flämische Arbeitsgemeinschaft)	26	1.71	31	1.17	57	1.37
VNV (Vlaamsch Nationaal Verbond)	156	10.29	563	21.39	719	17.34
NSJV (Nationaal Socialistiche Jeugd in Vlaanderen)	46	3.03	56	2.12	102	2.46
Unaffiliated	1,086	71.63	1,735	65.94	2,821	68.03
Grand totals	1,516		2,631		4,147	

These figures are interesting because they show that, contrary to what has often been stated, there was no polarisation of annexationists into the Waffen-SS and autonomists into the Legion. In fact, more members of the integrationist *Germaansche SS Vlaanderen* and *Devlag* joined the 'nationalist' Legion than the 'pro-German' Waffen-SS. This may have been due to the higher standards of fitness required by the Waffen-SS, or simply that SS bureaucrats sent recruits where they were most needed. The small number of National Socialists in the Flemish Legion was not unique, for according to German calculations, only thirty per cent of the Dutch legionaries came from the NSB. Yet in 1943 the VNV suspended its support for SS recruiting and enlistments in the newly formed Brigade 'Langemarck' immediately slowed.

Although the Germans had raised the legions to fight against the Soviet Union, their masters at home continued to envisage other roles for them. For example, they could be used as an instrument for carrying out a coup. They could be used to bolster up a shaky and unpopular collaborationist government. They could combat the growing threat of resistance, and could, as a last resort, defend their country from invasion. No wonder the collaborationist parties supported recruiting, and even ordered their members to volunteer.

Treatment of Germanic Volunteers

On paper the terms of service for Germanic and ethnic German members of the Waffen-SS and the Germanic legions appeared to be fair, and comparable with those of Reich Germans in the Wehrmacht and Waffen-SS. Dissatisfaction resulted when German agencies deliberately disregarded the conditions of service, or were prevented by wartime circumstances from observing them.

On arrival at SS training centres, many volunteers had their illusions rudely shattered. The Frederician discipline of the Waffen-SS came as something of a shock, but what was immediately apparent was the complete lack of trained SS instructors. Apparently no selection had taken place, nor had efforts been made by the SS authorities to prepare the training staff for the difficult task of dealing with foreigners and overcoming the language problem.

In all armies recruits are subjected to considerable verbal abuse, but when SS NCOs began to refer to the Flemings as 'a bunch of mercenaries who are only interested in their pay', or 'a nation of idiots', 'filthy people', or 'a race of gypsies', and muttered, 'if these are the best what are the rest like?', national susceptibilities were roused. The Flemings, with their 'Russian language', appeared to have born the brunt of abuse, but such treatment was meted out to all the legionaries irrespective of nationality.

In March 1942 the Flemish leader, Staf de Clercq, brought the matter to Himmler's attention. Himmler was incensed and ordered the sergeant-major to report to him in person – the officer responsible having been killed in action in the meantime. Himmler emphasised that correctness of behaviour towards Germanic volunteers was decisive for the Germanic future. He had already reserved to himself all appointments down to platoon commander *(Zugführer)* and company sergeant-major *(Stabsscharführer)*. Officers were to attend eight- to fourteen-day courses at the SS School in Sennheim or at the *SS-Hauptamt*, and before they left for the front Himmler wanted to meet them so that he could personally explain to them the heavy responsibility that they bore. Conditions did improve, but the Flemings had one more grievance which was not rectified until 1944. Many of the volunteers were devout Catholics, but they had joined an organisation that was non-Christian and officially *Gottgläubig*. Consequently, they were forbidden to have their own clergy or to attend Mass.

Danish and Finnish volunteers were insulated from the worst SS abuses by the presence of their own officers and NCOs. Following the release of surplus Danish officers, a further thirty-nine volunteers were discharged, possibly on the grounds that they had criminal records. Instead of being returned home, they were sent to German firms in Halle, where they were treated as forced labourers until their status was rectified.

A number of grievances were caused by the working of the German administrative machine. At first the organisation for paying allowances to the dependents of legionaries functioned slowly and caused hardship. A considerable delay and even non-delivery of mail was a result of handling by non-German postal officials who were inimical to the legions. In addition the SS Security Service, or SD, censored the mail for security reasons, and also because they wanted to sample legion morale and opinion in occupied countries. Often the next-of-kin of a legionary heard of his death from comrades before they received official notification from Berlin.

Flemish volunteers arrive at the SS Training Camp at Sennheim in Alsace

Staf de Clercq meets *SS-Sturmbannführer* Lettow-Vorbeck in Flanders preparatory to his taking command of the Flemish Legion; June 1941

The dining-hall at Sennheim

Left
Barrack-room fatigues at Sennheim

Right
The school commander at Sennheim congratulates a successful recruit; autumn 1941

Below
Sport played an important part in SS training. Here a boxing match takes place in the gardens at Sennheim

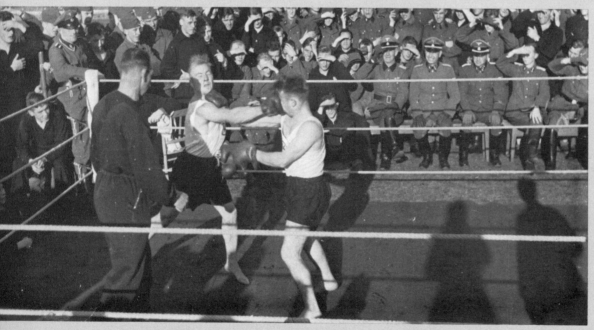

Deployment of Germanic Legions

German failure to destroy the Red Army in the summer of 1941 prolonged the campaign and made greater demands on German manpower than had been anticipated. By the end of November 1941 the Germans had lost 740,000 men, for whom there were only 400,000 replacements. The combing-out of manpower in the armies' rear areas did not produce sufficient men to make good this deficiency, with the result that the front-line infantry was deprived of a quarter of its strength even before the beginning of the hard battles of the winter. From then on, the Germans were obliged to employ makeshift measures to create new formations, as well as satisfy the immediate needs of the units at the front.

Had the German timetable gone according to plan, the foreign units would probably have arrived too late to have seen any serious action, but as it happened they provided a welcome reinforcement, even though their numbers were totally inadequate. In action at the front, the battalion, or at most regimental, sized legions created difficulties. As fighting units they lacked a 'tail', and so were logistically dependent on German formations. The heaviest weapons they possessed were infantry guns, and fire support, when needed, had to be provided by German artillery. The Legions could not be inserted between German formations at the front and be left to fight their own private war against Communism. They had to be placed tactically under the command of German formations. For example, 'Freikorps Danmark' served with the *SS-Totenkopf-Division* at Demyansk. For much of their existence the legions served under the two SS brigade headquarters, which were ill-provided with supporting arms, or alongside Baltic police units, which in many cases were even worse supplied with heavy weapons than the legions themselves.

By February 1943 the plight of the Germanic volunteers was a sorry one. Their losses had been heavy and only a trickle of replacements, from home or returning from convalescent units, kept them in existence. To make matters worse, the volunteers who had signed on for two years in 1941 would complete their term of service during the summer. This, coupled with poor

Waffen-SS men relax on capturing a village

At first SS tactics which relied on the swift attack, by small but lethal assault groups, supported by precisely co-ordinated and flexible back-up proved invincible against the uninspired and lumbering performance of the Soviet Army, but things did not remain that way for long

recruitment in the Germanic countries, caused the *Reichsführer-SS*, Heinrich Himmler, to decide to expand the Germanic SS-Division *'Wiking'* into an Army Corps of two divisions by incorporating what was left of the legions.

Felix Steiner provided an epitaph for the legions in the last order of the day to them: 'The steadfastness which you have shown on the northern sector of the eastern front is worthy of the proud traditions of your native countries. . . . The grenadiers of the great Prussian King could not have fought better, nor more bravely.'

All evidence suggests that the legions fought well, and as a consequence suffered heavy losses. There is no evidence to suggest that they were sacrificed to save German lives; on the contrary, they served closely with German ground forces, and shared the same risks and losses. Although it is not clear whether the SS-sponsored legions had a harder time than those organised by the German Army, all the Legions, however, irrespective of their sponsor, were at a disadvantage compared with German units. The German units had a reservoir of replacement manpower on which to draw to make good losses, while all the legions could hope for was that enough adults with right-wing sympathies could be persuaded to enlist.

SS losses in the invasion of the Soviet Union were difficult to replace, and this gave added impetus to the search for manpower abroad

Some of the civil population of the Ukraine looked to the Germans to liberate them from Bolshevik oppression, and at first treated the Germans as friends and liberators

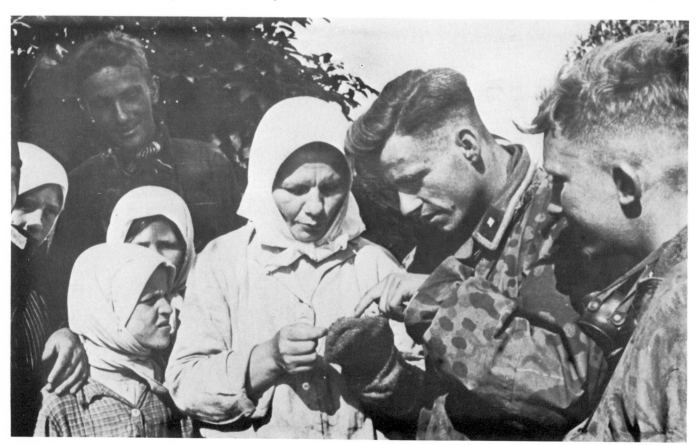

STORIES

The Forerunner–
Freiwilligenstandarte 'Nordwest'

As the number of convinced National Socialist volunteers from Scandinavia and the Low Countries began to dry up, and the SS encountered difficulties in finding suitable recruits for the SS Regiments *'Nordland'* and *'Westland'*, it decided to form a new type of volunteer regiment designed to appeal to a wider cross-section of young men with nationalist rather than National Socialist sympathies.

On 3 April 1941 the *Freiwilligenstandarte 'Nordwest'* was called into existence. As opposed to being of the SS, this new unit was to be with the SS. Its volunteers – having met the same racial and physical requirements – were to have the same rights and duties as SS men, but were not to be members of the Waffen-SS. An outward sign of this subtle distinction was the Waffen-SS uniforms with the SS runes replaced by a different device on the collar patch.

The establishment was set at 2,500 Dutchmen and Flemings. In its first month it received 920 volunteers, who were, in many cases, from the Dutch NSB and Flemish VNV. Although there is no doubt that *'Nordwest'* was formed to participate in the attack on the Soviet Union, its volunteers were naturally not told this vital piece of information. After training in Hamburg-Langenhorn, and taking the oath of the Germanic Waffen-SS (see Appendix 4), the Regiment was placed under the *Kommandostab Reichsführer-SS*. For all its imposing title, this headquarters was intended to 'mop-up' behind the rear of the advancing German Armies.

While still preparing for active service, the Regiment was split into *Freiwilligenverband Niederlande and Freiwilligenverband Flandern*. These two volunteer formations were to be established in Poland, at Krakow and Radom respectively, each having the strength of a horse-drawn infantry battalion. In effect this meant that *'Nordwest'* had become a regimental headquarters controlling the training of the nuclei of two separate volunteer legions. On 26 July 1941 it was announced that *'Nordwest'* was to continue as a proper tactical unit containing two battalions and its own regimental companies and supply column. In addition to the Dutch battalion in *'Nordwest'*, there was also to be a separate Dutch Legion in the strength of a regiment of three battalions.

A contingent of Flemish volunteers arrives at the SS barracks at Hamburg-Langenhorn; April/May 1941

On 12 July 1941 members of *'Nordwest'* swore a new oath of loyalty to Adolf Hitler, not as Führer, but as Supreme Commander of the Armed Forces, and only in the battle against Boshevism.

By 1 August *'Nordwest'* had 1,400 Dutchmen and 400 Flemings together with 108 Danes under training at Debica; another contingent of 405 Flemings arrived a few days later. Towards the end of the month, *'Nordwest'* and the new Dutch Legion began to move to another training area at Arys-Nord in East Prussia. However, it soon became apparent that there were insufficient recruits for both *'Nordwest'* and the Dutch Legion, and on 24 September 1941 the *SS-Führungshauptamt* announced a complete reorganisation. *'Nordwest'* was disbanded without having fired a shot in anger, and instead there was to be a regimental-sized Dutch Legion, and Flemish Legion in the strength of a reinforced battalion; both legions were to be completely motorised.

The name *'Nordwest'* reappeared later in the order-of-battle of the Waffen-SS, but contrary to what some post-war writers have said, the anti-tank companies and the guard battalion that bore this name had nothing whatsoever to do with the Germanic Volunteer Regiment.

A platoon of the 6th (Flemish) Company of *'Nordwest'* at rifle drill; Hamburg-Langenhorn, June/July 1941

SS-Untersturmführer Boulanger, one of the German officers of the Flemish Battalion of *SS-Freiwilligenstandarte 'Nordwest'*, during field exercises at Debica, Poland; autumn 1941

Clothing inspection for Dutch volunteers in the wooded camp at Debica in Poland; summer 1941

Freiwilligen–Legion Niederlande

Vrijwilligers Legioen Nederland

When the German armies poured into the Low Countries in May 1940, sensational reports of German parachutists landing behind the Dutch lines dressed in nuns' habits appeared in the newspaper headlines. Although far-fetched, the reports had a basis in fact. At the outbreak of war in September 1939 there were several thousand Dutchmen working in Germany, and many of those with pro-German sympathies were members of the Association of National Socialist Dutchmen in Germany, which had its own paramilitary organisation known as 'Sport and Recreation'. The German military intelligence organisation *Abwehr* recruited a number of Dutchmen for training, and sixty of them, dressed as Dutch railwaymen, soldiers, and gendarmes, seized bridges and other important objectives for the invading Germans. Although many were National Socialists, Anton Mussert, the leader of the Dutch NSB, was not consulted and knew nothing about the treacherous activities of his compatriots.

Dutch volunteers are given a noisy send-off at The Hague; 26 July 1941

Volunteers wait for a medical examination; Amsterdam, July 1941

Registration of Dutch volunteers in Amsterdam; July 1941

The first contingent of Dutch volunteers marches through The Hague. At their head is a colour party of Dutchmen from 'Nordwest' with the Dutch 'Beggars' flag' that was presented to the contingent by General Seyffardt; 26 July 1941

Dutch language recruiting pamphlet for the Waffen-SS and Dutch Legion which was issued in 1941

These first Dutchmen to take up arms for Germany came to the attention of Gottlob Berger, and he immediately established an SS recruiting office in The Hague. Already in May 1940 the recruiting of Dutchmen for SS Regiment 'Westland' was under way. The options offered to volunteers were the innocent-sounding 'six months' sports course' or the two- or four-year engagements. It appears that many Dutchmen thought they were volunteering for police work, and it was not until they began field training that they realised their mistake. This, coupled with undiplomatic German officers and unsympathetic German training staff, led some hundred Dutchmen (mostly members of the NSB) to be discharged for 'having the wrong attitude'.

Despite these set-backs, more than 1,000 Dutchmen had joined the Waffen-SS, 631 of whom were serving in Division 'Wiking'. By September the number had risen to 821, which was

Anton Mussert greets *SS-Oberführer* Otto Reich at an SS concert in The Hague; autumn 1941. Reich was a former Death's Head Regiment officer (note the cuff-band of his former regiment), and was neither a successful nor popular legion commander

probably due to the impetus provided to recruitment by the invasion of the Soviet Union. Meanwhile NSB support for 'Nordwest' meant that it now contained 1,400 Dutchmen, sufficient for Himmler to reorganise the Regiment to contain a Dutch battalion, in addition to the regimental-sized Legion. As it happened, enlistment forecasts were over-optimistic and as there were never sufficient volunteers for two full regiments, 'Nordwest' was wound up, and its Dutch personnel joined the Legion.

The German invasion of the Soviet Union aroused considerable interest in occupied Europe, and gave SS recruiters a welcome boost. In July 1941 the leader of the National Socialist Dutch Workers' Party, Dr Henri Ridder van Rappard, called on his countrymen to join the Waffen-SS, and on 10 July the German Commissioner for the Netherlands, *SS-Obergruppenführer* Seyss-Inquart, appealed for volunteers for a Dutch Legion, which had acquired a veneer of respectability when former Chief of the Dutch General Staff Lieutenant-General Seyffardt agreed to take charge of the Legion's organisation. Seyffardt hoped to keep the Legion out of politics, but Mussert saw it as a useful political weapon, and so tried to infiltrate it with his NSB members. Few apparently volunteered, and in April 1942 all members of the paramilitary formation of the NSB, the *Weer Afdeling*, were ordered to join the Legion.

The Commandant of the Dutch Legion, General Seyffardt, hands over a Dutch tricolour or 'Beggars' flag' to the first contingent of Dutch volunteers; The Hague, 27 July 1941.

At the headquarters of the Dutch Legion, General Seyffardt hands a pennant to the Commander of the *Weer Afdeling*, Zondervan. The pennant was then presented to the 1st (WA) Battalion of the 2nd Regiment of the Dutch Legion; 11 October 1941

On 11 October 1941 a battalion of Dutchmen left Amsterdam to join the earlier contingents already training in Germany. This new draft was referred to by Mussert and the NSB as the 'WA Bataljon', but officially it was the 1st Battalion of the 2nd Regiment of the Dutch Legion.

Earlier it had been reported that it was intended to form a complete Dutch Division, and the number of volunteers began to make it seem possible, but the moment the Dutch recruits reached their training area at Arys in East Prussia things began to go wrong. The twenty-three Dutch reserve officers led by Colonel Stroink were considered by the Germans to be both insufficient in number and inadequate in training, and so German officers were posted to the Legion. This immediately led to friction and the resignation of Stroink and five of his fellow officers. In the ranks things were no better, for many objected to swearing an oath of allegiance to Hitler. As the train carrying the WA contingent traversed Germany on its way east, it was passed by a train carrying 266 disillusioned Dutchmen back to Holland.

The result of these problems was an immediate falling off of recruits and the collapse of the infant 2nd Regiment; thereafter the Legion never succeeded in fielding more than one regiment. Even so, the Dutch was still greater than the Flemish, Norwegian, or Danish contributions. The 2,600 men serving in the Legion early in 1942 could have been even greater had the SS recruiters not been so fastidious. Berger still found time to discuss with Rauter (Senior SS and Police Commander in the Netherlands) the problem of repatriation of criminal elements who had wormed their way into the Legion.

From Arys the Dutch Legion travelled by sea via Danzig to Libau, and then by foot and motor transport to the northern sector of the eastern front, where it arrived in late January 1942. Its first action was at Gusi Gora on the Volkhov, north of Lake Ilmen, where, after a month of heavy defensive fighting, the Legion counter-attacked. In mid-March 1942 an additional Dutch Legionary unit – a reinforced field hospital – left its training area at Oranienburg for the eastern front. At the end of March the Legion was withdrawn, having lost eighty per cent of its strength, and having won the commendation of the *Oberkommando der Wehrmacht*.

The report of the officer responsible for setting up a replacement battalion for the Legion led Anton Mussert to demand the Legion's withdrawal from the eastern front. Losses on this scale would not endear him to the Dutch people; nor did he want to see his supporters in the Legion slaughtered. However, in any event the Germans could not consider disengaging the Legion at that time. After considering Mussert's demands, Berger and Rauter came to the conclusion that so many volunteers had come from outside Mussert's NSB, or had joined for non-political reasons, that Mussert could not claim to speak for a majority of legionaries.

Waffen-SS fire over the open sights of their anti-aircraft gun during the fighting in the Volkhov pocket

Dutch volunteers receive welcome food parcels from home. Second from left is *Leg.-Unterstumführer* Zondervan; summer 1942

Christmas on the Volkov front near Leningrad. The fact that 'Saint Nicholas' wears a war correspondent's cuff-band suggests that this congenial scene was set up for the photographer; December 1942

A Dutch dug-out on the Leningrad front. The sign incorporated both the German and Dutch SS symbols and the Dutch SS motto 'Hou en Trou'

A German NCO with the Dutch Legion in Russia (note absence of armshield); summer 1942

During the spring of 1942 the Legion was brought up to strength again, although not all the new intake were Dutchmen but ethnic Germans from North Schleswig. In the summer the Legion again formed part of Army Group North at Krasnoye Selo near Leningrad. On 15 June the Legion captured the commander and 3,500 members of the 11th Soviet Army, and continued to be engaged in heavy fighting for the rest of the year. By the end of the year – having lost forty-two men on 4 December alone – and despite periodic reinforcements, the Legion had been reduced to 1,755 men. Although still twice as large as the other Germanic legions and still capable of functioning as a regiment within the 2nd SS Infantry Brigade, one rifle company in each battalion was in a state of suspended animation.

For the Legion, 1943 began with hard fighting, and on 5 February it received the news that Lieutenant-General Seyffardt had been assassinated at his home by the Dutch resistance. Following severe fighting the legionary *Sturmmann* Gerardus Mooyman knocked out thirteen Soviet tanks and became the first Germanic volunteer to win the Knight's Cross of the Iron Cross. His sub-unit, the 14th (anti-tank) Company, was commended by the *Oberkommando der Wehrmacht*. On 27 April the Legion was extricated from the line and sent home on leave.

Himmler estimated that 1,700 Dutchmen would be available for the newly formed Germanic SS Panzer Corps, but many Dutchmen objected to joining the Waffen-SS, and refused to take the oath. It is not clear how many objected on conscientious grounds, and how many simply had no desire to do any more fighting. On 20 May 1943 the Legion was officially disbanded at Grafenwöhr in Germany.

On 5 February 1943 General Seyffardt was shot outside his home, and died the following day. On 10 February he was given a military funeral in the courtyard of the Ridderzaal at the Binnenhoft in The Hague

General Seyffardt's coffin draped with his personal standard, which was in the NSB colours and was charged with the four stars of his rank in the Royal Netherlands' Army; 10 February 1943

A Red Cross nurse hands out cigarettes to Dutch volunteers. In the distance the outskirts of Lengingrad, spring 1942

A Company Commander chats with one of his men in the defensive positions north of Krasnoe Selo, spring 1942

Leg. *Sturmmann* Mooyman and a comrade mark with white tape the number of kills on the barrel of their anti-tank gun, February 1943

Leg.-*Rottenführer* Gerardus Mooyman, the only legionary to win the Knight's Cross; 9 March 1943

Mooyman and his comrades of the 14th (anti-tank) company at a ceremony held at the front; 17 March 1943

Mooyman describes to the Commander of the 1st SS Infantry Brigade, *SS-Brigadeführer und Generalmajor der Waffen-SS* von Scholz, the action in which he won the Knight's Cross

The official portrait of *Leg. Rottenführer* Gerardus Mooyman. His other decorations are the so-called Russian Front Medal and Iron Cross 2nd Class ribbons in his buttonhole, and Iron Cross 1st Class on the left breast

Mooyman meets members of the Dutch press in Berlin during his visit there on 23 March 1943

Mooyman is received by the Senior SS and Police Commander, *SS-Gruppenführer* Rauter (left), and *Reich* Commissar for the Netherlands, Seyss-Inquart; April 1943

Freiwilligen–Legion Flandern

In the summer of 1940 the SS opened a recruiting office in Antwerp, and invited young Flemings to join the new SS Regiment *'Westland'*. No doubt Himmler expected that young Flemish National Socialists would volunteer in the same way as their counterparts in the other Germanic countries. It was not unreasonable to assume that those Flemish nationalists who envisaged a union of the Netherlands and Flanders would welcome the opportunity to serve in a Dutch-Flemish regiment. But when, in February 1941, Berger quoted the numbers of Germanic volunteers in the Waffen-SS he did not mention any Flemings; nor did *SS-Division 'Wiking'* include any Flemings among its 1,143 Germanic volunteers just prior to the invasion of the Soviet Union. By September 1941 there were still only forty-five Flemings serving in the Division.

The reason for the lack of Flemings lay in the relationship between the German government and the *Vlaamsche Nationaal Verbond*. In the autumn of 1940 the political branch of the SS was formed in Flanders. Known variously as the *Algemeene Schutscharen Vlaanderen, Vlaamsche-SS*, or *SS-Vlaanderen*, it immediately began to poach members of the VNV's own militia – the Zwarte Brigade. The leader of the VNV, Staf de Clercq, Naturally resented this and attacked the Flemish SS in speeches and in the press to such an extent that it hampered the work of the Flemish SS, and thus recruitment for the Waffen-SS which it was supposed to assist.

On 26 April 1941 Berger agreed to stop the efforts of the SS in recruiting members of the *Zwarte Brigade* if Staf de Clercq would cooperate with the SS. Staf de Clercq was prepared to recruit members of his party and its paramilitary formations himself, on condition that they served in *'Nordwest'* and not in the Waffen-SS proper. He probably hoped that in the less rigid environment of *'Nordwest'*, his members would not be so indoctrinated with National Socialism that they would be lost to the cause of Flemish nationalism. This agreement did not prevent Berger from recruiting Flemings who did not belong to the VNV, and so there were other sources of manpower in the fervently pro-German *Deutsch-Flämische Arbeitsgemeinschaft* (German Flemish Labour Group), the *Vlaamsche Oudstrijders*, and the *Rex-Vlaanderen*.

Departure of the first contingent of the Flemish Legion after presentation of a colour at the Palace of Fine Arts in Brussels on 6 August 1941. The colour party was made up of Flemings from *'Nordwest'*, and the contingent was commanded by *SS-Untersturmführer* Boulanger with, on his left, Jef François

By 1 August 1941 400 Flemings had joined 'Nordwest', and its three Flemish companies (numbered 1, 6, and 8) were despatched to Radom under the designation *Freiwilligenverband Flandern*. There it was intended to organise them into a horse-drawn infantry battalion. Meanwhile a further draft of volunteers left Antwerp on 27 September 1941 and were sent to Debica, where they were joined by the Flemish Infantry Battalion. The two contingents were merged and moved to Arys in East Prussia to complete their training. The force was now known as *Freiwilligen Legion Flandern* and comprised a headquarters and headquarters company, two rifle companies, one machine-gun, one mortar and one anti-tank gun company.

In the autumn of 1941 the Legion was hastily motorised and sent to the Leningrad front, where from 16 November it was engaged in heavy defensive fighting, following which it served on the Volkhov front. In the New Year the Legion repelled ferocious Soviet counter-attacks north of Novgorod. For its conduct in these engagements the Legion was cited by the XXXVIII Army Corps, and by the *Oberkommando der Wehrmacht*.

Flemish volunteers leave the Gare du Nord in Brussels at the beginning of their journey to Radom in Poland; 6 August 1941

At the beginning of March 1942 the Flemings mounted an attack on the Soviet lines, but had to be extricated after six days because of heavy losses. An officer of the Dutch Legion, which had been serving in the same sector as the Flemings, went home on leave early in April and reported that the Flemish Legion had been reduced to seventy men.

The first commander of the Legion, *Sturmbannführer* Michael Lippert, was wounded during the fighting in the Volkhov pocket and had to be evacuated. *SS-Sturmbannführer* Josef Fitzthum assumed temporary command, while the nephew of the famous German colonial general, *SS-Sturmbannführer* Hans Albert von Lettow-Vorbeck, visited Flanders in preparation to take up command of the Legion. It so happened that the Danes were desperately in need of a commander, and Lettow-Vorbeck, after only a short time at the front, was sent to them instead. Fitzthum handed over command of the Legion to its last commander, *SS-Hauptsturmführer* Conrad Schellong, in July 1942.

Flemish volunteers at drill in their camp at Arys in East Prussia

Reimond Tollenaere, the commander of the Flemish Black Brigade, fell in action at Kopzy as an *SS-Untersturmführer* in the Flemish Legion. The bronze badge was instituted to commemorate his death

A Flemish machine-gun crew move-up during the defensive fighting in the northern sector of the eastern front; December 1942

Flemish volunteers learn to use the 8cm mortar

From June to November 1942 the Flemish Legion was commanded by *SS-Sturmbannführer* Fitzthum, seen here as an *SS-Brigadeführer* with Himmler at Neuhammer, Silesia; 12 January 1944

SS-Standartenführer Michael Lippert photographed after his recovery from the severe wounds he received as commander of the Flemish Legion

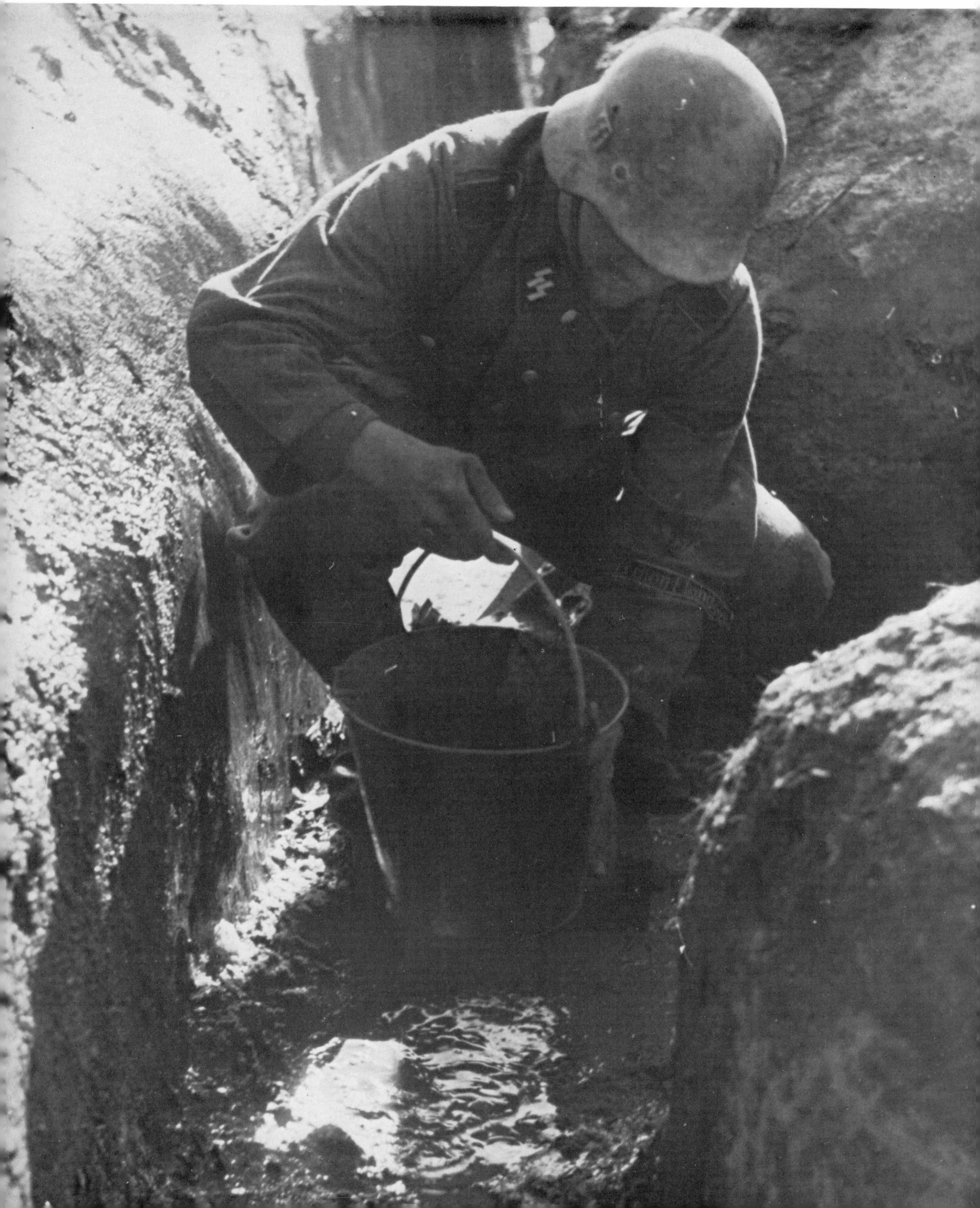

The end of June and most of July 1942 saw the Legion mopping up Soviet survivors in the Volkhov pocket, and the Flemish volunteer, Julius Geverts, was awarded the Iron Cross 1st Class, the first awarded to a Flemish legionary. The Legion then moved to the Lengingrad front where it was employed in defensive fighting in the Stara Panovo–Finev Lug area until early August. Next it served south of Kolpino, and then, leaving one company behind, went into brigade reserve in Krasnoye Selo. In February 1943 the Legion went into Corps reserve at Federvskoye, before participating in defensive fighting on the bend of the Neva. During the second half of March 1943 the Legion served under the 24th and 254th Divisions in Nikolskoye, Badeyev, and finally south of Krasny-Bor. In less than a week's fighting the Legion's 1,116 men had been reduced to fewer than sixty men.

After six weeks in reserve at Szablino, the survivors were withdrawn to Debica in Poland in May 1943. As in the other legions, there were a number of legionaries who had had enough of fighting and refused to swear a new oath which was required of them. They were sent to the Legion's depot in Breslau. There were a number of plans for the remaining Flemings, but they were too grandiose for the number of volunteers still serving or willing to join a new formation. Instead of forming an infantry regiment for the SS Police Division, the Flemings were eventually used to form an independent formation of a new type – an Assault Brigade *(Sturmbrigade)* which was called 'Langemarck,.

Conditions in the trenches on the Leningrad front were reminiscent of those during World War I; spring 1943

The Flemish Legion arrives at the banks of the Neva; January 1943

SS-Sturmbannführer von Lettow-Vorbeck was just long enough on the eastern front as commander of the Flemish Legion to decorate his men with the Tollenaere Commemorative Badge; June 1942

Hauptsturmführer Rehmann, former deputy commander of the Flemish Legion, Jungclaus, Himmler's Plenipotentiary for Belgium and northern France, *SS-Sturmbannführer* Schellong (former Legion commander), Dr Jef van de Wiele, chief of De Vlag, *SS-Haupsturmführer* Schleich (of Jungclaus's staff), and Flemish SS regimental commander *SS-Untersturmführer* Jef François

Flemings prepare to carry food containers across a river to troops in defensive positions; Russia, spring 1942

A *Leg.-Sturmann*, wearing regulation insignia in the correct positions, prepares a demolition charge; Russia, February 1944

Freikorps Danmark

Frikorps Danmark

Only a few hours after the German attack on Denmark on 9 April 1940 the King and his government realised that it was futile to try to resist, and sued for peace. The German government 'took the Kingdom under its protection rather than occupying it', and Danish institutions and Army remained virtually intact.

The first Danes to enlist were those who joined SS Regiment *'Nordland'* just a few weeks after the German invasion, and these were in the main members of the Storm Troops *(Storm Afdeling-en)* of the Danish National Socialist Workers Party (DNSAP). Soon, however – despite the opening of recruiting offices in Copenhagen and four other towns – enlistments petered out. By February 1941 Berger estimated that there were only 200 Danes in the whole Waffen-SS, and in September, despite the filip given to recruiting by the invasion of the Soviet Union, the Danish contingent in *SS-Division 'Wiking'* still numbered only 251 men.

On the initiative of the Foreign Secretary, Erik Scavenius, Denmark broke off diplomatic relations with the Soviet Union on 26 June 1941, and encouraged those Danes who had fought in the Finnish Army during the winter war of 1939–40 to think of reconstituting the *Dansk Finnlands Bataljon*. However, Finland was short of both weapons and equipment and was unwilling to take untrained volunteers. On 23 June the leader of the DNSAP, Frits Clausen, launched an appeal for volunteers for Regiment *'Nordland'*, but a few days later word reached Denmark that Himmler had agreed to the formation of a Danish Battalion within Division *'Wiking'*.

The first appeals for volunteers were launched on 27 June 1941, and by the 29th eight recruiting and twenty-four reporting offices were operating in Denmark. The participants in the conference at the German Foreign Office were informed that, as of 30 June, a Danish Free Corps, independent of Regiment *'Nordland'*, was already in existence, and on 2 July it was announced that the Danish force was to belong to the Waffen-SS, but it was not to form part of Regiment *'Nordland'*. Three days later the German press announced that the new Danish Free Corps was in need of Danes with recent military experience, and on 8 July the Danish War Minister permitted regular and reserve

Departure of the first
volunteers for the
'Freikorps Danmark'.

Danish National Socialists canvas for volunteers for the 'Freikorps Danmark'. The placards exhort Danes to 'Fight under the Danish Flag against Bolshevism', 'Against the pest over Europe' and 'We will win with the "Freikorps Danmark"'

Departure of the first contingent of volunteers for the 'Freikorps Danmark' from Hellerup station destined for Hamburg

The imposing entrance to the SS barracks in Hamburg-Langenhorn

Arrival of the first contingent of Danish volunteers at the SS barracks in Hamburg-Langehorn; 20 July 1941. The colour bearer was *Kornet* Mathey Wagner

Danish volunteers, still wearing their 'Nordwest' collar patch, swear the oath of allegiance to Adolf Hitler at a ceremony in the SS barracks which was attended by the Senior SS and Police Commander 'Nordsee', SS-Gruppenführer Querner; 2 July 1942

personnel of the Danish Army to enlist in the *Frikorps*. Shortly after this the War Minister changed his mind and decided that all Danish military personnel who joined the *Frikorps* would be discharged from the Danish Army and would forfeit their pension rights. This was a serious set-back and Berger hastened to Copenhagen; after numerous negotiations the Germans prevailed on the Danish War Minister to guarantee the seniority and pension rights of Danish volunteers.

On 3 July 1941 an advance party of 150 Danes left Denmark for the SS barracks at Hamburg, where on 15 July the *SS-Führungshauptamt* ordered the establishment of the *Freiwilligenverband Dänemark*. The nucleus was to be provided by one Danish officer and 108 Danes from Volunteer Regiment 'Nordwest'. On 20 July they were joined by a Staff and 1st Battalion with 480 men. By 31 December 1941 the strength had reached 1,066 men, and 1,164 by early 1942.

The appearance of official backing given by the Danish government to the establishment of the Free Corps encouraged a number of Danish Army officers and men to enlist; far more, in

A Dutch recruiting poster

WIE van deze twee IS
Legion Niederlan
DE WARE NEDERLANDER?
manche

MELDT U AAN : bij de **WAFFEN-SS** of bij het **VRIJWILLIGERSLEGIOEN VLAANDEREN**

ERSATZKOMMANDO FLANDERN DER WAFFEN-SS - ANTWERPEN, KONINGIN ELISABETHLEI, 22

UITGAVE : ERSATZKOMMANDO FLANDERN DER WAFFEN-SS

Flemish recruiting poster for the Waffen-SS or Flemish Legion with the exhortation 'Flemings up!'

fact, than in any of the other Germanic legions. But this led to problems when Berger, who expected the volunteers to be National Socialists, found that the first commander, Lieutenant-Colonel Kryssing, insisted that the Free Corps existed solely to combat Bolshevism. The Germans then tried to remove Kryssing, and these intrigues led to a delay in the training programme. Eventually, on 8 February 1942, Kryssing was moved to an administrative post on the grounds that an artilleryman could not be expected to command an infantry battalion. Kryssing recommended a Captain Schock, but he was unacceptable to the SS because he was a freemason. Finally, a Captain-Lieutenant in the Danish Royal Life Guard, and a youth leader in the DNSAP, Christian Frederik von Schalburg, was transferred from the 'Wiking' Division. Schalburg, who was of Baltic-German extraction, was soon killed at the front, while Kryssing soldiered on to become the first Germanic officer to become a Waffen-SS general.

Legions-Obersturm-bannführer Kryssing, first commander of the *Freikorps Danmark*

S S-Sturmbannführer von Schalburg, his son Alex, and *Leg. Unterscharführer* Søren Kamm, who was later to become the only Danish holder of the Knight's Cross

The SS barracks at Posen-Treskau which was the home of the Freikorps from September 1941 until May 1942

At the end of August 1941 the *Freikorps* was augmented by a signal section *(Bataillons Nachrichten Staffel)*, and in September it was converted into a motorised infantry battalion. On 13 September the *Freikorps* moved to Treskau, near Poznan, where an *Ersatzkompanie* was formed to provide replacement personnel. With the completion of training the German training staff was dissolved.

On 8 and 9 May 1942 the *Freikorps* was transported by air from Heiligenbeil in East Prussia via Pleskau to Demyansk where it was placed under the *SS-Totenkopf-Division*. From 20 May to 2 June the *Freikorps* joined the fight to destroy a Soviet bridgehead which threatened the vital road link to the German pocket at Demyansk. During an attack on 2 June the commander, von Schalburg, was wounded in the leg and then killed by an artillery salvo. His second-in-command, *SS-Hauptsturmführer* Knud Borge Martinsen, assumed command and ordered a withdrawal. As the assault companies pulled back, they left their commander and twenty-four comrades buried beside the road near Biakovo.

During the night of 3–4 June 1942, the *Freikorps* was transferred to the northern side of the corridor, from where the Soviets, despite determined attempts, were unable to dislodge it. By the 6th the Danes had been relieved, and while encamped in woods near Vassilievschtshina, a number of volunteers received the Iron Cross from the hands of their commander. On 10 June

Leg. Haupsturmführer Per Sørensen was commander of the 1st Company of the *Freikorps* during the bitter battles of July 1942. He was killed during the battle of Berlin on 24 April 1945

From May to October 1942 the *Freikorps* served under the *SS-Totenkopf-Division*. Here a Danish volunteer greets members of the SS-T-Division. The photograph confirms that the *Dannebrog* was sometimes worn on the sleeve by members of the *Freikorps*

Insulated from the crowd by members of the DNSAP, German military police, and families and friends, the *Freikorps*'s progress through Copenhagen was marked by occasional cheers and frequent brawls

1942 Martinsen was superseded by *SS-Obersturmbannführer* Hans Albert von Lettow-Vorbeck, nephew of the legendary defender of German East Africa. This was resented by the Danes, who considered it a breach of the agreement reached with the Germans that the *Freikorps* was a Danish unit with its own officers. Additionally, in the short time that he held command, Martinsen had proved more than able to lead the battalion.

On the very day that Lettow-Vorbeck arrived to take command, the Red Army launched a surprise attack and regained Bolshoi Dubovitsky. By midday the situation had grown so serious that he was obliged to order a withdrawal. Although twice wounded, Lettow-Vorbeck was trying to reach his forward company when he was killed. Martinsen took over, and succeeded in extricating the *Freikorps*. That evening, what remained of the *Freikorps*, its rifle companies reduced from seventy to forty men each, was relieved. While it was resting in new defensive positions near Vassilievshtshina, replacement personnel arrived from Poznan, and Martinsen was promoted to *SS-Sturmbannführer* and confirmed as the *Freikorps* commander.

The memorial service for Christian Fredrik von Schalburg was attended by members of the Danish Royal family and government, and senior German officers and officials

The Red Army launched a major attack on 16 July and captured Vassilievshtshina, thus cutting off the vital road link with Demyansk. Throughout the 17th the *Freikorps* was subjected to continuous air and tank attack. By the 23rd the Germans, with

After the disbandment of the *Freikorps*, the cuff-band was proudly worn on other uniforms by former members

the *Freikorps* on the left flank, succeeded in retaking Vassiliev-shtshina and re-opening the road. For their role in this engagement the *Freikorps* was mentioned in the order-of-the-day of the German 28th Rifle Regiment. On 25 July the Danes went into reserve where they were joined by their heavy company.

Between May and August 1942, the *Freikorps* had lost seventy-eight per cent of its strength, and so on 5 August the unit was ordered to leave the Demyansk area and return to its former barracks at Mitau, before taking four weeks' leave in Denmark. On arrival in Copenhagen the *Freikorps* marched through the capital to the Old Citadel where they were to be billeted, but the parade was not a success and the progress of the unit was marked by occasional cheers and frequent brawls, which continued throughout the leave.

On 12 October the *Freikorps* reassembled in Copenhagen and returned to Mitau, where training began again in earnest. Martinsen, meanwhile, attempted to instil some National Socialist spirit into the Danes. By 5 December 1942 the *Freikorps* – reinforced from its replacement company – had been placed under the command of the 1st SS Infantry Brigade for operations south of Velikiye Luki. After three uneventful weeks in reserve, the *Freikorps* was attacked by a Soviet NKVD (Internal Security Troops) Division on Christmas Eve and thrown out of the village of Kondratovo. On Christmas Day the Danes counter-attacked and regained the village. On 16 January 1943 the German pocket in Velikiye Luki surrendered, and the *Freikorps* was moved north to the Moschino-Kondratovo sector where, on 25 February, it attacked and seized a Soviet strongpoint at Taidy. This was to be the *Freikorps* last battle, and on 20 March 1943 it was ordered to travel by train to Grafenwöhr in Germany.

The 650 survivors were first sent on leave, not collectively as before, but in batches in order to avoid the incidents that had occurred the previous autumn. On their return, and despite unwillingness to join anything but a purely Danish unit, most of the Danes transferred to the Waffen-SS and a new Danish Regiment. The *Freikorps* was officially disbanded on 6 May 1943.

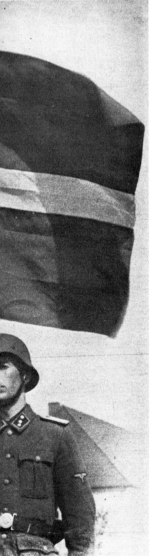

The colour of the *Freikorps Danmark;* Hamburg-Langenhorn, 2 July 1942. The colour was taken to Russia and later returned to Copenhagen in September 1942, but what happened to it thereafter is not known

NORDMENN

KJEMP FOR NORGE

Meld deg i Stortingsgata 12 · OSLO

Freiwilligen–Legion Norwegen

Den Norske Legion

Soon after the conquest of Norway the SS established a recruiting office *(Ergänzungsstelle 'Nord')* in Oslo, and began to recruit Norwegians into the SS Regiment *'Nordland'*. Although basically sympathetic to SS recruitment, Vidkun Quisling, leader of the Norwegian National Party *(Nasjonal Samling),* had reservations. He certainly did not want to see his country become a *Gau* of the Germanic Reich as advocated by the SS, but by manning the Legion with his party members he hoped to gain influence and eventually power for his party and himself.

SS recruiting propaganda in Norway was couched in rather nebulous National Socialist terms, but did claim that German intervention had foiled a British plot to occupy Norway. On 13 January 1941 Quisling broadcast an appeal for volunteers for Regiment *'Nordland'* to participate in 'the war of freedom and independence against English despotism'. Even after the commando raid on the Lofoten Islands, few Norwegians could have felt threatened by Britain, and when another collaborator, Jonas Lie, revived ancient claims to the Orkney and Shetland Isles and the Outer Hebrides, they found it difficult to take them seriously.

After initial successes, recruitment figures fell to such an extent that the SS had to lower its standards. At first only unmarried men between seventeen and twenty-five years were accepted, but by April 1941 the SS was considering married men up to the age of forty. On the eve of the invasion of the Soviet Union, Division *'Wiking'* could muster a mere 294 Norwegians (excluding those serving in other SS units). Three months later, and after suffering casualties, *'Wiking'* still had only 291 Norwegians. The impetus given to SS recruiters by the invasion of the USSR had only served to balance the losses.

In Norway there were a number of men who were unwilling to join the SS, but who were prepared to fight alongside the Germans against the Bolsheviks. As in Denmark there were men who had hastened to the aid of Finland during the Winter War of 1939-40, and were keen to rejoin on the resumption of hostilities between these two countries. On 28 June 1941 the Norwegian adviser on legal matters to the German administration, Sverre Riisnaes, was quoted as saying that there was nothing to prevent

Recruiting poster for the Norwegian Legion: 'Norseman fight for Norway. Report to Stortingsgata 12, Oslo'

Norwegian volunteers from joining the Finnish forces. On the following day the *Reichskommissar* for Norway, Josef Terboven, and the *Nasjonal Samling* announced the formation of a national Norwegian force. This led to the belief that the Norwegian Legion had been established to help the Finns, and no doubt accounted for the initial surge of volunteers.

Another boost was provided by the Norwegian writer and Nobel Prize Winner, Knut Hamsun, who was pro-German and considered that the Legion was essential for the future of Norway. Hamsun was not, however, a National Socialist, and although the Legion was not supposed to have been affiliated to any political party, a large number of its members were either sympathisers with the *Nasjonal Samling* or came from its paramilitary wing, the *Hird,* or from the infant political branch of the SS in Norway, the *Norges-SS*.

During July 1941 Norwegian volunteers were gathering in the Bjølsen Skole at Galskogen, and on the 29th the first 300 left Norway for Germany. They disembarked at Kiel and travelled to the manoeuvre area at Fallingbostel. Here the Norwegian Legion was officially established on 1 August 1941. The first commander was Captain Jørgen Bakke, a Norwegian, but he soon resigned as a result of disagreements with the German authorities.

On 3 October 1941 the 1st Battalion of the Norwegian Legion was sworn in at a ceremony in Fallingbostel, which was attended by Vidkun Quisling, *SS-Gruppenführer* Jüttner, head of the *SS-Führungshauptamt* (on his left), and *SS-Gruppenführer* Rediess

The Norwegian Legion's first commander was *Leg.-Sturmbannführer* Jørgen Bakke, seen here with his adjutant at the swearing-in ceremony; 3 October 1941

A chosen number of volunteers symbolically swear on their colour, while the remainder take the oath in their ranks

The Legion grew in strength from 700 on 2 August to nearly 2,000 on 20 October 1941. Early in 1942 the *SS-Hauptamt* gave the Legion's strength as 1,218. By the time the Legion reached the Leningrad front on 16 March 1942 it had a strength of 1,150 men with a further 150 in training. The Legion's second commander was *Legions-Sturmbannführer* Arthur Quist.

It was originally intended that the Legion should consist of a regimental headquarters and headquarters company, a war-correspondents' platoon, an infantry battalion, and a cyclist unit. The infantry battalion contained the normal three rifle companies and one machine-gun company, all of which were dependent on horse-drawn transport. The *Radfahrabteilung* comprised two squadrons, one motorised telephone section, and four motorised wireless sections. Replacement personnel for the Legion were to be provided by an un-numbered *Ersatzbataillon* at Holmestrand near Oslo.

The second commander of the Norwegian Legion was *Leg.-Sturmbannführer* Arthur Quist, who survived the war to be captured by the Norwegian resistance in May 1945

A Norwegian sentry outside the 4th company office of the Norwegian Legion at Fallingbostel

During a visit by Vidkun Quisling to Germany, the 1st Battalion was sworn in at a ceremony in Fallingbostel on 3 October 1941. This battalion was also known as the *Viken* Battalion, having taken its title from a *Hird* regiment of the same name. Early in 1942 a police company, destined to be the first of four, was raised in Norway, and left for the eastern front in October 1942.

On 5 February 1942 the German High Command announced that it was unable to send the Legion to Finland because of transport difficulties. Instead the Legion was to be sent to join the *2. SS-Infanterie-Brigade (mot.)* on the Leningrad front. The Norwegians moved through Riga to within a few kilometres of Leningrad, where they soon became involved in patrols and small raids. German field post office numbers suggest that the Norwegian Legion gradually began to be whittled away. The first to go were the regimental headquarters and its company, which suggests that the Germans had given up hope of getting sufficient Norwegians to form a regiment. The personnel were probably used to form a 14th (anti-tank) Company. The cyclist unit disappeared, and the replacement battalion was reduced to a company in September 1942, although another new replacement company operated in Jelgava (Mitau) in German-occupied Latvia from the beginning of 1943.

The Norwegian Police Company leaves Oslo for the eastern front near Leningrad; 1942

Norwegian volunteers arrive at their billets on the northern sector of the eastern front near Leningrad; August 1942

Much of the area around Leningrad was swamp with birch tree forests. Here a wounded Norwegian is carried to a field dressing-station; spring 1943

Recruiting handbill for the Danish Freikorps: 'For Denmark against Bolshevism'. Report to SS Recruiting Command Denmark, Kobenhavn V Jernbanegade 7

For most of its existence the Norwegian Legion fought in the northern sector of the eastern front where it suffered heavy casualties. As early as May 1942 it was reported that most of the unit had been wiped out, and this prompted Quisling to visit the survivors at the front, where they were serving in I Army Corps of the German 18th Army. Replacements were badly needed, and in October Berger wrote to Himmler saying that a more 'neutral' form of propaganda was being tried out and that a disguised recruiting office had been established in Oslo. Reports from the front had been circulated to the press and as a result 2,200 men from the *Nasjonal Samling* had applied and were being examined. The *Ersatzkommando* hoped to dispatch 500 men in November, and a further 500 at the beginning of 1943; however, only 317 of the 478 men processed were examined, and out of these 19 joined the Waffen-SS, 114 went to the Legion, while 103 remained with the *SS-Wachbataillon* in Oslo. Berger pointed out that recruiting for the Waffen-SS was being adversely affected by an intensive campaign on behalf of the Legion. In October Gottlob Berger had to cope with an attempt to filch some of 'his' Norwegians by the German Navy, which proposed to use them as frogmen and on coastal defence. A row ensued between Berger, Terboven, the Navy, and finally Himmler, which was never resolved. When, in autumn 1943, the Navy again tried to recruit Norwegians, the Legion no longer existed.

FOR DANMARK!
MOD BOLCHEVISMEN!

**Meld Dig hos ⚡⚡-Ersatzkommando Dänemark
København V., Jernbanegade 7**

Reichsführer-SS Himmler and *Legions-Sturmbannführer* Jonas Lie, who commanded the 1st Police Company on the eastern front until its return to Norway on 6 April 1943

With the Waffen-SS and the Norwegian Legion against all enemies ... against Bolshevism

A pen and ink study of night fighting on the eastern front by Norwegian SS war correspondent Wigforss

Late in 1942 the Norwegian Legion briefly served with the 1st SS Brigade in Army Group Centre, where it carried out security duties alongside the Danish Free Corps in Belorussiya. Before the end of the year it returned to the 2nd SS Brigade on the northern front, where it was engaged with heavy losses in the defensive fighting at Krasnoye Selo, Konstantinovka, Uretsk, and Krasny Bor.

The depleted but still cohesive Legion was withdrawn to Jelgava (Mitau) in February 1943, where Himmler inspected the 800 men still serving. Since February 1942 the Legion had suffered 158 fatal casualties. In March 1943 the survivors were sent home on leave. In May 1943 Quisling called on the remaining legionaries to join a new Norwegian Regiment, and 600 men – the nucleus of the 1st Battalion of the Regiment 'Norge' in the new Germanic SS Division – swore the oath of the Waffen-SS. On 20 May 1943 the Norwegian Legion was disbanded at Grafenwöhr, and those Norwegians who had no wish to soldier on in the Waffen-SS, or serve in a unit which was not purely Norwegian, were released and sent home.

Russians in occupied territories used to make walking-sticks and other souvenirs which they would barter for food with the occupiers. Here a Norwegian volunteer carves for himself a 'Volkhov' stick; spring 1943

At a Norwegian reception held in the Kaisersaal at the Zoo in Berlin, Norwegian volunteers fraternise with Norwegian girls in national costume; 10 January 1942

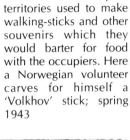

The Volunteer Replacement Battalion of the SS

Before departing for the front, each of the Germanic legions formed a replacement or *Ersatz* unit. As in the Army and Waffen-SS, the main purpose of this unit was to receive, document, and equip new recruits, who were then trained and held until the parent field unit required replacements. Other tasks of equal importance were the care and re-training of convalescents discharged from hospital, and the maintenance of records of those killed in action. Through the depot passed all those discharged for one reason or another. The replacement unit therefore acted as a reception centre, training unit, holding unit, and records office.

At first it was planned that each Legion should have its own replacement unit, but a few weeks after their establishment, they were combined for administrative convenience under a battalion headquarters in the SS Barracks at Radom in Poland. This new unit was known as the Volunteer Replacement Battalion *(Freiwilligen Ersatzbataillon SS)*. In addition to the legions, this new unit served the Finnish Volunteer Battalion. By the beginning of December 1941 the Replacement Battalion headquarters had moved to Wetzelsdorf near Graz in Austria.

The next reorganisation took place in December 1941 when it was renamed *Ersatzbataillon der Legionen* and organised in four companies; the first serving the Danish Free Corps, the second the Flemish, the third the Dutch, and the fourth company the Finnish Battalion. The Norwegian Legion had its own Replacement Battalion at Holmestrand near Oslo, and had to call on Graz for its German cadre only. It was intended eventually to provide a replacement battalion for each legion but there were never sufficient recruits. The plan to form a Dutch Replacement Battalion in early 1942 was never carried out. Shortage of recruits meant that the Norwegian Battalion was reduced to a company in September 1942, by which time it had moved to Mitau. With effect from 1 January 1943 a second replacement company joined the first. The moves of the Norwegian Company to Mitau, and the Danish Replacement Company to Bobruysk were dictated by the need of these replacement companies to be

Two views of the newly-built SS barracks at Graz Wetzeldorf

The new SS barracks at Graz-Wetzeldorf; winter 1941

nearer to their parent unit at the front. In December 1942 a Convalescent Platoon was formed for the Danish Free Corps and immediately moved to Breslau.

The complete re-numbering of Waffen-SS units and formations meant that, in the spring of 1943, the Replacement Battalion of the legions became *SS-Panzer-Grenadier-Ausbildungs und Ersatzbataillon 11*, which because of the imminent disbandment of the legions was intended to serve the Germanic SS Panzer Corps. The Flemings were not affected by this redesignation because they had their own replacement company, which left Graz to join the SS Grenadier Replacement Battalion *'Ost'* in Breslau.

Epilogue

The Germanic SS Panzer Corps

By February 1943 the so-called Germanic *SS-Panzer-Grenadier-Division 'Wiking'* had been severely mauled, and even a thorough comb-out of its tail had not made any appreciable difference to its fighting potential. The Division was clearly in need of a rest and refit.

Even as early as April 1941 the shortage of new recruits for Regiments *'Nordland'* and *'Westland'* had caused their replacement battalions to be amalgamated. Heavy casualties during the first Russian winter had meant that *'Nordland'* had to use what was left of its third battalion as replacements for the other two, and take the Finnish Battalion as a new third battalion. At the beginning of 1943 the volunteers who had signed on for two years were coming to the end of their engagements.

Flemish volunteers (de Smet and Lauf) serving in Regiment *'Westland'* in Klagenfurt. The wings or 'swallow's nests' denote a member of the corps of drums

Himmler now felt that the time was right to expand *'Wiking'* and the legions into a new Army Corps of two divisions. This was to be accomplished by a complicated juggling act. The Norwegian contingent and a German cadre were to be taken away from *'Wiking'* to form the nucleus of a new division to be called *'Nordland'*. The remaining Finns and Germans in the old Regiment *'Nordland'* were to form a new Germano-Finnish Regiment to be called *'Kalevala'*. Regiment *'Germania'* was to remain in *'Wiking'* and would include Danes, Estonians, Finns, Liechtensteiners, Flemings, Dutchmen, Swedes, and Swiss. Regiment *'Westland'* was to continue as *'Wiking's* light infantry regiment.

The new division *'Nordland'* was to be organised like *'Wiking'*. One of the Panzer Grenadier Regiments was to be called *'Danmark'* and contain Danes from *Freikorps Danmark* and those attending a course at Sennheim, with any shortages being made good with Germans. The other motorised infantry

SS-Brigadeführer und Generalmajor der Waffen-SS von Scholz congratulates members of the anti-tank company of the Dutch Legion. Note both patterns of cuff-band being worn simultaneously

regiment was to have been Dutch in composition, but Mussert objected. The new light reconnaissance Regiment was to be called 'Norge'. Its two battalions, derived from the Norwegian Legion, were to be brought up to strength by Norwegians from Sennheim and Germans. Himmler envisaged that the Division's tank, artillery, and technical units would be composed of Reich or ethnic Germans, the latter coming from the German minority in Romania.

When Mussert heard that Dutchmen were to serve in a division called 'Nordland' he objected so strongly that it was agreed that the Dutch contingent would form the nucleus of a new *Panzer-Grenadier-Brigade* of two regiments to be called 'Nederland'. This was not entirely due to Mussert, since the SS planners reached the conclusion that a Dutch Brigade would ensure that the new Panzer Corps would have two mobile formations under its command, since Division 'Wiking' could not be extricated from the front to join the new Corps.

The Flemish Legion was to be expanded into a regiment as the nucleus of an Assault Brigade to be called 'Langemarck', as well as providing personnel to other divisions; but not for the new Panzer Corps – presumably to make certain that Flemings did not come into contact with the Dutch Regiment.

The French-speaking Walloon Legion which was to be transferred from the German Army to the Waffen-SS was to provide a motorcycle battalion for the new Corps, while its 'best' racial specimens were to go to Regiment 'Germania' and other supporting elements of 'Wiking'. One set-back was the loss of the Finnish contribution, in June 1943.

Meanwhile, the Estonian Legion was providing a battalion of men for the Division 'Wiking' (SS-Panzergrenadier Bataillon 'Narwa') as well as additional personnel for the divisional engineers and other units.

Execution of this grandiose plan, which, if successful, would have given Himmler a formidable force of two Panzer Divisions, each with two motorised infantry regiments, one tank regiment, one mobile *(Schnelles)* infantry regiment, and ancillary units, was only partly realised. The great stumbling block was not equipment but personnel. The dissolution of the legions was resented by the many volunteers, who were willing to serve in national units, but not in the pan-Germanic Waffen-SS. Those nearing the end of their two-year engagement were indifferent because they could serve out their term in offices or training units. But those who had signed on for four or more years were simply posted where they were required without being consulted. When called to swear an unconditional oath some refused, but were later coerced into doing so. A small number of recusants were discharged. There is no way of ascertaining how many of the two-year men would have re-engaged had the legions continued. Nor is it possible to tell how many civilians might have volunteered had the legions not been disbanded.

The Reckoning

The first foreign volunteers to fall into the hands of the enemy were those captured by the Soviet Army in the Baltic, East Prussia, and Berlin. The Russians do not appear to have differentiated between the Waffen-SS men and those from other branches of the armed forces, nor were SS men segregated in special camps. The Soviet attitude was simply one of expediency: every able-bodied prisoner was to carry on living only in so far as he contributed to the reconstruction of the Soviet Union. He was kept alive to expurgate his 'crimes' by hard manual labour. By the tenth anniversary of the victory over Fascism those who survived had all been repatriated.

In the West SS men were usually segregated, held in captivity slightly longer than their comrades in the other branches of the armed forces, and given harder and more dangerous jobs, such as mine-clearance. They were also singled-out for particularly harsh treatment but, once it was realised that not all SS men (or those who wore SS uniform) were war criminals, conditions did improve. In fact not a single legionary or foreign member of an SS combatant unit was formally tried and executed in Western Europe simply because he served in the legions or Waffen-SS, apart from three dubious cases in Holland in 1945 in which espionage played a role. Most were given fairly lenient terms of imprisonment, which were soon followed by a free pardon.

A greater problem for the military collaborator was not surviving the defeat, but winning the battle for rehabilitation once he was released from prison. In many cases his home had been looted on VE day, or later comandeered by the State. If his wife or family had not been arrested as accomplices, they would almost certainly have been ostracised, and his children barred from attending the local school. As a collaborator he was not entitled to any form of pension or social assistance, nor was it easy to find a job, especially for the disabled. But the years spent in the SS, the hardships endured at the front and in prison after the war, had forged these veterans into a fairly self-sufficient brotherhood. They formed associations, operated their own welfare organisations, and kept in touch via newsletters. A few of these have now grown into magazines (see bibliography), and regular meetings are held, often in the face of local opposition.

Most post-war governments realised that if former collaborators were not given every chance to re-integrate themselves into society, an embittered and potentially disloyal element would perpetuate itself. So a governmental campaign was launched to encourage people to forgive if not forget, and steps were taken to punish those who continued to discriminate against former collaborators. But many found it impossible to begin life again in their old homes. They moved to districts where their past was unknown, while others emigrated to the United States, Canada, South America, Spain, and one or two to Britain. Others went to live in Germany where their term of service in German uniform was more appreciated and where, after a considerable delay, former members of the legions and Waffen-SS were finally awarded a pension.

There is no doubt that at first it was thought that the purest form of treason was the taking up of arms in the service of one's country's enemies, but opinion gradually changed. Although useful to German propaganda, the military contribution of the legions to the German war effort was not great. Nor did this form of collaboration have any direct bearing on the civil population left at home to endure the occupation. Much more hated were the informers, 'horizontal collaborators', and economic collaborators (black marketeers) who deprived their countrymen and made fortunes by providing the enemy with the services, produce, and industrial goods denied to the civil population. It has also been argued that the legions—by their very existence—prevented the Germans from carrying out some of their more extreme occupation policies.

On the other hand the military collaborators were not really repentant. They viewed the worsening relations between the West and the Soviet Union with satisfaction, and saw it as a justification of their deeds. They tended to regard themselves not as criminals facing a judge, but as losers delivered in chains at the feet of the victors.

The judges who tried the collaborators soon came to the conclusion that the military collaborators were by no means the worst. Professor Langemeyer, the Solicitor-General at the Dutch Supreme Court for Collaboration wrote: 'The greatest experience of these Courts of Justice has been to find that a person who has fought on the side of the enemy, can yet be, all in all, more a good man than bad, and also not be a fool. This experience accounts for the fact that the military collaborators received relatively light sentences, and not, as was generally expected in the beginning, the death penalty.'

This change of attitude, and the fact that many of these soldiers were mere youths, and had certainly not profited from the occupation made forgiveness easier, and rehabilitation more prompt.

Holland

At the end of the war the surviving Dutchmen who had served in the Dutch Legion or the Waffen-SS were to be found in military hospitals in Soviet occupied territory, Soviet prison camps, or in camps in Holland. By June most of those taken prisoner in Holland had been concentrated in two main camps at Veluwe, and the former German concentration camp at Vught. Those taken prisoner by the Red Army were returned in 1950 and 1951.

The SS prisoners in Vught were dressed in striped concentration camp clothing and subjected to the same brutalities and indignities as the former inmates. These conditions prevailed until the Dutch government was able to supervise the running of the camp and provide suitable guard personnel. Generally speaking, conditions in other camps were acceptable considering the shortages and difficulties facing the country as a whole.

Conditions in Veluwe camp were certainly better according to the Dutch journalist Ton van Weert who visited the camp on 15 June 1945: 'I have visited 4,000 young Dutchmen in one of our well-known army camps in Veluwe. It has been a long time since I met such a large number of my compatriots in such excellent physical condition. But . . . their uniforms are German! Their insignia are those of the Waffen-SS, with badges such as 'Legion Nederland,' 'Wiking', and 'Landstorm Nederland'. For the time being they are prisoners-of-war of the Canadian Army. Soon they will be prisoners of the Dutch people and will have to answer to charges of treason or worse. Densely packed they stand around me. They are extremely correct and very well trained. But their voices show their emotion very clearly: 'Do you know what is going to happen to us?' '. . . the bullet or the rope?'

To pass sentence on these soldiers, as well as the many thousands of other collaborators, special courts were established, and the death penalty re-introduced for the first time since its abolition in 1873. Punishments ranged from death (215 sentenced but only 36 carried out) to imprisonment, fines, forfeiture of property, and deprivation of civil rights. Those who had served in the the Waffen-SS were banned from military service in Holland, while at least 60,000 Dutchmen (including 20,000 wives) who had been in the service of the German armed forces (including the Waffen-SS) or the German State lost their Dutch citizenship.

Anton Mussert was executed by firing squad on 7 May 1946, while the Dutch *Ritterkreuzträger* Gerardus Mooyman was sentenced to six years' imprisonment, but was released after serving only two years. None of the former Dutch officers who had sworn an oath of allegiance to the Dutch Crown were actually executed for treason, although many, like Stroink, were sentenced to death only to be later pardoned.

Flanders

The Belgian government in London had been discussing the post-war treatment of collaborators since 1942 but, when liberation finally came, neither it nor the Military Government in Belgium were prepared to deal with the 70,000 who had been rounded-up by the Resistance.

Those members of the Flemish Legion still serving in the Waffen-SS retreated from the Oder river, and surrendered to the Americans near Schwerin on 2 May 1945. From there they were sent to the former German concentration camp at Neuengamme, which was being used by the British as an SS cage. In the autumn the Flemings were handed over to the Belgian Army who transported them by cattle truck to the Belgian Army camp at Beverloo. This first contingent consisted of 1,900 men and four Flemish Red Cross nurses. On arrival at Beverloo station the prisoners were allegedly kicked and beaten the three miles to the camp. A survivor noted that it appeared as if a national holiday had been called and half the Belgian Army was there. Once inside the camp the prisoners were subjected to the same brutalities, indignities, and lack of medical attention as the inmates of a German concentration camp.

Subsequently 65,000 persons were charged with having been members of various German or pro-German armed formations. From 1944 to 1947 4,170 people were sentenced to death, of which 3,193 had been charged with military collaboration. By December 1949, when the camp at Beverloo had been closed down, only 230 executions had been carried out, often in front of as many as a thousand eager spectators.

Denmark

By 28 May 1945 more than 12,000 people had been arrested for collaboration in Denmark. Arrests were proceeding at the rate of a hundred a day in Copenhagen alone, where the authorities were urgently considering the building of special camps. In June the death penalty—abolished in 1895—was restored and 112 death sentences passed. But by April 1948 only 28 had been carried out.

Those Danes who survived the last months of the war on the eastern front were taken prisoner by the Red Army, the last of whom were returned to Denmark in November 1953.

The status of members of the *Freikorps* was a delicate issue in post-war Denmark. At one stage the Danish War Minister had consented to the enlistment of Danish military personnel into the *Freikorps*, but later changed his mind. After the war Danish volunteers were tried as collaborators, but claimed that they had been led to believe that the *Freikorps* had the backing of the Danish government. The government replied that even if it had it

The *'Freikorps Danmark'* war memorial at Hovelte, which was blown up by the Danish resistance in May 1945

Close up of the role of honour of fallen members of the *Freikorps*, which includes the name of one of the White Russians who served in the *Freikorps*

was not a valid excuse, since the volunteers should have realised that the government was acting under German pressure. The authorities then proceeded to cancel the volunteers' pension rights. Most volunteers were sentenced to one or two years' imprisonment.

Frits Clausen, the leader of the Danish Nazi Party, died of a heart attack while awaiting trial in prison. The first commander of the *Freikorps*, and later SS General C. P. Kryssing, still lives quietly in retirement in Denmark. K. B. Martinsen was executed on 25 June 1949.

Norway

The few Norwegians still serving in the Waffen-SS at the end of the war were virtually wiped out in Berlin, alongside their Danish and French comrades.

In May 1945, 12,000 'Quislings' were arrested in the first surge of liberation, but during the summer about 8,000 were found to have been wrongly arrested and were released. However, the final total of 'Quislings' arrested was in excess of 50,000, which for a country of only 3,000,000 inhabitants was a not inconsiderable number.

The death penalty abolished in 1870 was re-introduced and 25 people were executed—including Vidkun Quisling who faced a firing squad on 24 October 1945. The former Chief of the Norwegian Police and Police Company Commander Jonas Lie died of a heart attack while awaiting trial. The Norwegian Legion commander Arthur Quist was arrested by the Home Front (Resistance) and sentenced to ten years' imprisonment. The average sentence passed on former members of the legion was three to four years' imprisonment.

Arthur Quist was captured at the former Gestapo headquarters in Hamar, May 1945

Part III LEGIONARY

Foreign Volunteer Uniforms

While the legions were in the process of formation during the summer of 1941, discussions were still in progress as to the legal status, uniforms, and ranks of foreign volunteers in the German forces.

After a discussion on this subject in June 1941, Hitler decided that Norwegian volunteers were to be grouped together in a Norwegian Legion, and similar formations to be known as legions were then to be formed from Croats, Spaniards, and Italians.

The first volunteers had automatically assumed that they would fight against Communism dressed in their own national uniforms, but this presented the Germans with a number of practical problems – from the simple one of identification of ranks, to the more complex ramifications of international law. Hitler had already agreed to the introduction of the standard German field-grey uniform. General Jodl agreed that the German national emblem would have to be worn on the sleeve, as in the Waffen-SS, otherwise, according to international law, Norwegians wearing Norwegian uniforms could be regarded as *franc-tireurs*, especially as Norway was a state with which Germany was technically still at war.

At a further conference at the German Foreign Office in July 1941, the international ramifications of recruiting foreign nationals was discussed. The Foreign Office was anxious about the suggestion that foreigners should retain their national uniforms because there was a danger that even if they wore German rank badges, they would not be recognised as members of the German Armed Forces. Gottlob Berger pointed out that this problem did not apply to the volunteers already serving in the Waffen-SS because they already wore German uniforms and rank badges, as well as a national badge.

It was finally agreed that German uniforms would be issued to all foreigners, and that their nationality would be identified by special national badges.

Foreign Volunteer Insignia

Having decided that foreign volunteers would wear German and not national uniforms, the SS planners turned their attention to insignia. The normal procedure was for the *SS-Hauptamt* to produce designs or prototypes for Himmler's approval. Once this was given, the *SS-Führungshauptamt*, in cooperation with the *SS-Wirtschaftsverwaltungs Hauptamt*, assumed responsibility for the manufacture and issue of these badges to the troops through the normal supply channels. What happened in practice was that the *SS-Führungshauptamt*, the legions' sponsors, and the legionaries themselves all had different ideas.

Where personnel received German uniforms in their homeland, insignia were often manufactured locally and, as in the case of the Dutch and Norwegian Legions, did not conform to the SS pattern. Volunteers who were clothed in Germany often received standard Waffen-SS uniforms with no special insignia, and volunteers had to improvise a national badge as best they could. Consequently, especially at the beginning, but also throughout the short history of the legions, one finds many different badges. In some cases different drafts of volunteers for the same legion wore completely different insignia.

At first most legionaries were wearing the following insignia:

Country	Cuff-band inscription	Collar patch device	Armshield
Denmark	'Freikorps Danmark'	Three-legged sunwheel, *Dannebrog,* or SS runes	None
Flanders	No cuff-band	Three-legged sunwheel or SS runes	Flemish lion
Holland	'Legion Niederlande'	Vertical wolf hook or SS runes	National flag in various shapes, sizes, and colours
Norway	No cuff-band	None	National flag

On 17 November 1941 the following insignia were authorised:

28. Uniforms and Badges of the Volunteer Legions (SS-FHA.-Kdo. Amt d.W-SS – I Leg./Az.64/11.41/Ge/F. von 17.11.41).

Cuff-band	Collar patch	Lower sleeve
Freikorps Dänemark	SS runes	National shield
Freiw.-Leg. Flandern	Sunwheel	Flemish lion
Freiw.-Leg. Niederlande	Wolf hook	National shield
Freiw.-Leg. Norwegen	Viking ship	Norwegian lion
Finn. Btl. der W-SS	SS runes	Finnish lion

Members of the replacement battalion wore their legion's particular insignia. Special insignia on the cap or helmet were not allowed.

However, the above order appears to have had little effect on what was then actually being worn:

Country	Cuff-band inscription	Collar patch device	Armshield
Denmark	'Freikorps Danmark'	Three-legged sunwheel, *Dannebrog*, or SS runes	National shield (but only rarely)
Flanders	'Frw. Legion Flandern'	Three-legged sunwheel or SS runes	Flemish lion
Holland	'Frw. Legion Niederlande'	Vertical and horizontal wolf hook or SS runes	National shield
Norway	'Frw. Legion Norwegen'	Norwegian lion or SS runes	National flag
Finland	No cuff-band	SS runes	Finnish lion

A Flemish cadet with, contrary to regulations, a numeral on his shoulder straps

It will be noted that certain inconsistencies appear in the inscriptions on the cuff-bands. The volunteers wanted the name of their country in their vernacular, but Himmler obviously preferred German. The Dutch rendering of 'Nederlande' probably originated in the 17 November 1941 order, and appears to have been changed at some later date, because original examples of this cuff-band exist with the German rendering 'Niederland'. In the case of the Danish Free Corps, a compromise appears to have been reached by adding the German *'Freikorps'* to the vernacular Danmark.

In June 1942 Himmler wrote to the chief of the *SS-Führungshauptamt,* Hans Jüttner, saying:

'I have considered for a long time the question of insignia for the Germanic legions, as well as for our Germans and ethnic-Germans, who though not fit for SS membership, are suitable for war service, and I have come to the following decision:

1. Personnel in Germanic legions will wear the following badges on their collar patches:
    a. Dutch Legion   Wolf hook
    b. Norwegian Legion   Norwegian emblem ('I am not sure what it is'*)
    c. Danish Legion   Danish lion†
    d. Flemish Legion   Flemish lion†

2. Above all I order all officers, NCO's, and men who are serving in a Germanic legion or volunteer unit to wear the same collar patch. SS members will then wear the SS runes on the left breast, like those SS members who are also policemen.'

The strict observance of the second paragraph by Germans serving in the Germanic legions depended, to a great extent, on whether their first loyalty was to the SS or to their unit.

On Waffen-SS uniform, distinctive insignia consisted of the right collar patch, the cuff-band, which was worn on the left cuff, and the armshield, which was worn on the left sleeve. These insignia were usually worn only on the tunic and greatcoat, and were not supposed to have been worn on drill, protective, or camouflage uniforms.

*Himmler's comment. †never issued

In August 1943 selected Germanic volunteers were sent to a special Germanic War Cadets' Course at the SS Officers' Academy at Bad Tölz. The legionary movement was now at an end and officers were desperately needed for the new Germanic SS Panzer Corps. These frame enlargements from a propaganda film about *SS-Junkerschule Tölz* show an interesting cross-section of legionary insignia; August 1943

A Norwegian cadet from the Norwegian Legion. On his breast pocket is the membership badge of Quisling's *Nasjonal Samling*

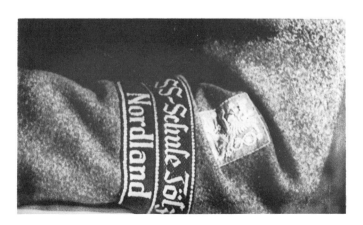

Collar patches

The collar patches for all ranks up to and including SS or *Legions Obersturmbannführer* was a black cloth parallelogram measuring 40 mm x 55 mm. The device on the right patch was usually machine-embroidered in silver-grey rayon. The collar patch with SS runes for officers was often hand-embroidered in aluminium wire, but collar patches with national devices were rarely manufactured in anything other than the standard machine-embroidered pattern described above. Few of the surviving wartime examples have manufacturer's marks or the issuing label of the *Reichszeugmeisterei*. The following collar patches are known to have existed:

Collar patch device	Introduced	Manufacture
SS runes	1933	German
Three-legged sunwheel	3.4.1941	German
Viking ship prow	30.7.1941	German
Vertical wolf hook	by 9.8.1941	Dutch
Horizontal wolf hook	17.11.1941	German
Dannebrog	12.7.1941	German
Norwegian lion in metal	1941	Norwegian
Norwegian lion machine-embroidered	1942	German

The November 1941 order laying down the insignia for the legions clearly states that 'special badges on the cap and steel helmet are not permitted'. Photographic evidence confirms that, in this respect, the order was complied with.

Cuff-bands

These were worn by all members of units or formations which had been awarded a cuff-band. It was worn on the lower left sleeve. In case of transfer to a unit with a cuff-band, the cuff-band of the former unit was replaced by that of the new unit. If the new unit did not have a cuff-band, the old cuff-band could continue to be worn.

The cuff-band was a woven rayon tape between 25 mm and 30 mm wide, with a 2 mm wide stripe along each edge which was composed of between twelve and fifteen metallic threads. The average issue length of the cuff-band was 490 mm. The name of the unit was either hand-embroidered in metallic thread, or machine-embroidered in silver-grey rayon for other ranks. In 1939 hand-embroidered cuff-bands for officers began to be replaced by a woven pattern, and in June 1943 the *Reichszeugmeisterei* announced that it could no longer supply hand-embroidered cuff-bands. The following cuff-bands are known to have existed:

Cuff-band inscription	Introduced	Manufacture
'Legion Niederlande'	by 9.8.1941	Dutch (very poor quality)
'Freikorps Danmark'	17.11.1941	Not known
'Freikorps Danmark'	17.11.1941	RZM manufacture
'Frw. Legion Niederlande'	17.11.1941	RZM manufacture
'Frw. Legion Nederland'	17.11.1941	RZM manufacture
'Frw. Legion Flandern'	17.11.1941	RZM manufacture
'Frw. Legion Norwegen'	30.7.1941	RZM manufacture

The cuff-band of the Finnish Volunteer Battalion was designed but never worn.

Armshields

Opposite
Recruiting poster for the Dutch Legion: 'Fight together under our own Flag against Bolshevism'. This shows the circular collar patch device which was in fact never worn

Facing page 121

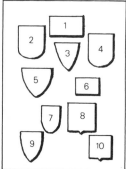

1. Dutch Legion. 1st improvised pattern
2. Dutch Legion. 2nd pattern variation made in Holland
3. Dutch Legion. 2nd pattern made in Holland
4. Dutch Legion. Regulation German pattern
5. Danish Freikorps. Regulation German pattern
6. Norwegian Legion. 1st improvised pattern made in Norway
7. Flemish Legion. Variation made in Belgium
8. Finnish Volunteer Battalion. Regulation German Pattern
9. Flemish Legion. Regulation German pattern
10. Finnish Volunteer Battalion. Variation made in Finland

The main purpose of the armshield was to identify the nationality of the wearer. At first there was no standard pattern, and each nationality received a differently shaped shield or national flag. The Danes at first wore their national flag on the collar patch, and were in fact the only nationality to do this. The Dutch were issued with a Dutch-made shield in the NSB colours. The Norwegians wore their national flag on the left sleeve. The German version of the Finnish shield was less popular than the heraldically correct red shield with golden lion that was manufactured in Finland. It was not until 1943 that a standardised set of shields – uniform in shape and size – was introduced for foreign volunteers in the Waffen-SS. At first the armshield was worn on the lower left sleeve 15 cm above the cuff-band, but both the Dutch and Norwegians wore their armshields under the SS national emblem on the upper left sleeve.

German-made armshields were all machine-embroidered on a black cloth ground which differed in shape, and varied in size from 55 mm to 60 mm high by 45 mm to 60 mm wide. The foreign-made badges differed in size and in manufacture. The following armshields are known to have existed:

Country	Type	Manufacture	Maker	Introduced
Norway	Flag	Woven	Norwegian	30.7.1941
Denmark	Shield	Machine-embroidered	German	17.11.1941
Flanders	Shield	Machine-embroidered	German	17.11.1941
Holland	Flag	Embroidered	Dutch	7.1941
	Shield	Hand-embroidered	Dutch	by 8.1941
	Shield	Hand-embroidered	Dutch	by 8.1941
	Shield	Machine-embroidered	German	17.11.1941
Finland	Shield	Hand-embroidered	Finnish	
	Shield	Machine-embroidered	German	17.11.1941

The German-made shields were manufactured by the old-established Berlin firm of Tröltsch und Hanselmann.

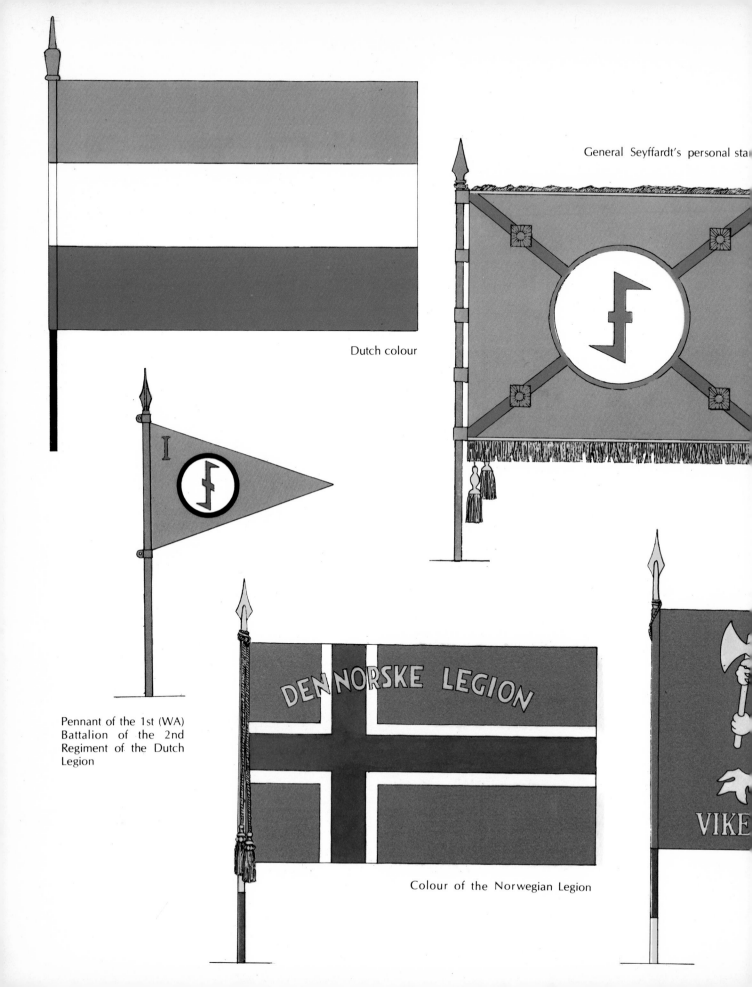

Dutch colour

General Seyffardt's personal sta

Pennant of the 1st (WA)
Battalion of the 2nd
Regiment of the Dutch
Legion

DEN NORSKE LEGION

VIKE

Colour of the Norwegian Legion

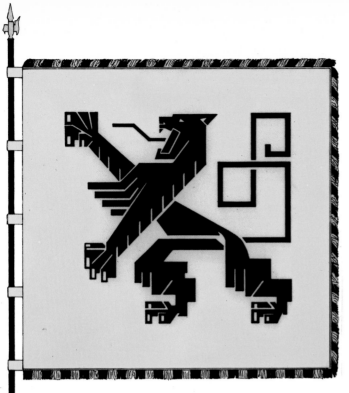

Colour of the Flemish Legion

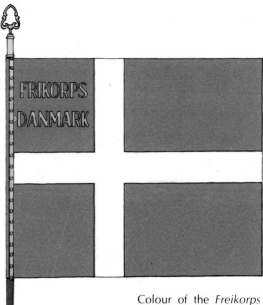

Colour of the *Freikorps Danmark*

Colour of the 1st *'Viken'* Battalion of the Norwegian Legions

Colour of the 1st Police Company of the Norwegian Legion

Colour of the Finnish Volunteer Battalion of the Waffen-SS

SS Freiwilligen–Standarte Nordwest

Collar patch introduced in April 1941 for all ranks. This collar patch continued to be worn by those who later joined the Flemish Legion and the *Freikorps* Danmark

Cuff-band introduced in July 1941 for all ranks. This is an issue machine-embroidered pattern

Freiwilligen–Legion Niederlande

Collar patch worn by first contingent of Dutch volunteers in *Freiwilligen Verband Niederlande*. This is, in fact, the standard Waffen-SS runic collar patch which was not supposed to have been worn by Germanic legionaries

Dutch-made collar patch worn by officers in the Dutch contingent. This particular example is **hand**-embroidered

Dutch-made collar patch worn by the contingent of Dutch volunteers which paraded in The Hague on 7 August 1941. The device is the vertical 'wolf hook'

Improvised arm badge worn by the first contingent of Dutch volunteers. No details concerning the provenance of this badge are known. The example illustrated is a replica

Dutch-made armshield which was worn by all ranks in the Dutch contingent. The badge is hand-embroidered in light blue, white, and orange thread on a black cloth backing

A draft of volunteers wearing the Dutch-made insignia with armshield under the SS national emblem, instead of in the regulation place just above the cuff-band; August 1941

Dutch-made cuff-band for all ranks in the Dutch contingent. This crudely made band was of black ribbon, with machine-embroidered white thread inscription and stripes

1

2

3 Frw.Legion Niederlande

4 Frw.Legion Niederlande

5 Frw.Legion Nederland

6 General Seyffardt

1 Regulation German-pattern collar patch introduced in November 1941. The device is the horizontal 'wolf hook' and is machine-embroidered in silver-grey thread

2 Regulation German-pattern armshield introduced in November 1941. This example is machine-embroidered in the correct Dutch national colours; reddish orange, white, and Nassau blue. For some reason the German-made shield is divided diagonally bendwise sinister, whereas the Dutch-made shield is divided diagonally bendwise

3 Regulation German-made cuff-band for officers. This is machine-woven in metallic and black rayon threads. This pattern is extremely rare, and this is the only known example (James van Fleet Collection)

4 Regulation cuff-band for other ranks introduced in November 1941. This is the standard machine-embroidered pattern with German spelling 'Niederlande'

5 The second pattern cuff-band for other ranks with the Dutch spelling 'Nederland'. It is conceivable that this pattern cuff-band was introduced at Mussert's insistence.

6 Cuff-band for all ranks in the 1st Company of the Dutch Legion. This example is the so-called 'BeVo' woven pattern which began to be manufactured at the end of 1942. The original award citation read as follows:

81. Presentation of Name

The *Führer* has with effect from 9 February 1943, awarded the 1. Company of *Freiwilligen-Legion Niederlande* the name 'General Seyffardt'. Soldiers of the *Freiwilligen-Legion Niederlande* are pledged to honour the murdered General Seyffardt on account of his anti-Bolshevik and Germanic convictions SS-FHA./Amt II/Org.

However, it is considered unlikely that this cuff-band was ever actually issued and worn before the enlargement of the Legion into a Brigade

The regulation German-made insignia being worn in the correct positions by two Dutch volunteers

Freiwilligen-Legion Flandern

1 Collar patch introduced in April 1941 for all ranks in the *SS-Volunteer Regiment 'Nordwest'*, and retained as the collar patch of the Flemish Legion

2 Armshield for all ranks. This machine-embroidered badge of German manufacture measured 55m×47mm, and was worn on the lower left sleeve

3 Armshield of Flemish manufacture. It was woven in yellow and black rayon thread and measured 55mm×41mm. This and many other items of Waffen-SS insignia are believed to have been made at factories in Ghent and Beverloo

4 Cuff-band for all ranks. This is the standard RZM pattern with machine-embroidered inscription

Two members of the Flemish Legion in Russia in March 1943. The lack of armshields suggests that these are not Belgian nationals. The *Leg.-Sturmann* on the left also appears in the next photograph wearing the sunwheel collar patch, while his comrade wears the SS runes

123

Freikorps Danmark

1 Collar patch introduced in April 1941 for all ranks in SS Volunteer Regiment 'Nordwest', and retained for a short time by those transferred to the *Freikorps Danmark*. It was authorised as the *Freikorps* collar patch on 12 July 1941

2 Collar patch for all ranks authorised by order of 28 April 1942. This was the only SS collar patch to incorporate a national flag, and may have been the original reason why Danish volunteers so rarely wore the national armshield. However, this collar patch was worn only for a short time during training in Hamburg

3 Armshield authorised on 17 November 1941 for all Danes serving in the *Freikorps*, but very rarely worn. This regulation example is machine-embroidered and measures 54mm × 53mm

4 First pattern cuff-band for all ranks. This unusual woven cuff-band with gothic inscription was probably manufactured in Germany, judging by its similarity to Hitler Youth cuff-bands. Photographic evidence suggests that it was far more common than the RZM pattern

5 Cuff-band for all ranks. This is the standard RZM pattern with machine-embroidered inscription

A member of the *Freikorps* wearing the *Dannebrog* collar patch

Dispatch rider Svend Aage Nielsen wearing the unusual pattern *Freikorps Danmark* cuff-band

Freiwilligen–Legion Norwegen

1 First pattern collar patch for all ranks. This was, in fact, the plain collar patch to which was added a white metal Norwegian lion. It was done by the Norwegians themselves because they apparently objected to the pattern with the Viking ship prow *(Schiffsteven)*, on the grounds that it perpetuated the sea-robber image, which they did not appreciate. Some time after June 1942 the collar patch with a machine-embroidered lion appeared in regulation SS manufacture. The example illustrated is a reconstruction

2 National flag worn by all ranks on the upper left sleeve. This badge was originally procured in Norway, and came in a number of different sizes and makes—the most common of which was woven and measured 40×55mm. The example illustrated is not an original

3 The badge of Saint Olaf's Cross was worn by all ranks who were members of the Norwegian *Nasional Samling* Storm Troops *(Rikshird)*. The badge illustrated has a diameter of 53mm and is woven in black and metallic thread for officers. The other ranks' version was the same size, but woven in black and grey-green rayon thread

4 Cuff-band authorised in November 1941. This is the standard RZM pattern with machine-embroidered pattern (Per Mork Collection)

A *Leg.-Oberscharführer* wearing the regulation SS-pattern collar patch with Norwegian lion device. Some contingents of the Norwegian Legion were issued with mountain troop clothing, either because they were kitted-out by *Kampfgruppe Nord,* or because the mountain cap and trousers closely resembled those of the former Norwegian Army

Colours

The Commander of the Dutch WA, Zondervan, having just handed over the pennant to the 1st (WA) Battalion of the 2nd Regiment of the Dutch Legion; The Hague, 11 October 1941

The first draft of Flemish volunteers with their colour, which had just been presented to them in the Palace of Fine Arts in Brussels; 6 August 1941

New volunteers swear on the colour of the Norwegian Legion

The colour of the 1st *'Viken'* Battalion of the Norwegian Legion at the swearing-in ceremony held at Fallingbostel on 3 October 1941. The battalion was named after the 1st Regiment of the *Hird* (the Norwegian *Nasjonal Samling* paramilitary formation). The motto *'Alt for Norge'* (All for Norway) and the dates of five battles fought between 1808 and 1814 appeared on the reverse of the colour

In September 1942 the first of four Norwegian Police companies was presented with a colour by Vidkun Quisling before departing for Germany

On 15 October 1941 the Finnish Volunteer Battalion of the Waffen-SS was sworn in on a colour which had just been presented to them by the Finnish Military Attaché in Berlin, Colonel Walter Horn; Gross Born on the Baltic coast, October 1941

Colonel Walter Horn, himself a former member of the Finnish *Jäger* Battalion in the Prussian Army during World War I, hands over the colour to the Finnish Battalion; Gross Born, 15 October 1941

Appendices

1 Finnisches Freiwilligen Bataillon Der Waffen-SS

The recruitment of foreigners into the Waffen-SS was noted in Finland, and, according to Berger, by December 1940 more than 100 Finnish subjects had expressed their willingness to join the German Armed Forces. Although the Finns were not strictly Germanic, Berger was desperate to find another source of volunteers and so concentrated on the minority of Finns of Swedish origin who did meet the racial requirements of the SS.

At the beginning of 1941 Berger received reports from the German military attaché in Helsinki that there were indeed potential volunteers. Berger was anxious to begin recruitment immediately, but two sovereign states were involved. Hitler gave his blessing to the project, and on 22 February the German Foreign Office entered into negotiations with Finland. The lack of urgency shown by the Foreign Office led Berger to go directly to the Finnish ambassador in Berlin and propose that an SS recruiting team go to Finland and select 700 volunteers. The Finnish ambassador was agreeable but could do nothing because Berger had circumvented normal channels. Berger, however, was not to be deterred and he persuaded a Scandinavian expert in the Foreign Office to draft an instruction to the German ambassador in Helsinki, which Ribbentrop approved. The terms of service were as follows: 1,000 Finns, at least half of whom were to have military experience, were to be recruited as 'workers for German industry'. Officers and NCOs were to have equivalent rank in the SS, and all ranks were to have dual nationality.

Further delays were caused by Finnish insistence that it was unseemly for Finns to serve alongside volunteers from countries occupied by Germany, and that it would be preferable for Finns to serve in the German Army rather than in the SS. It was obvious that the Finnish government had severe misgivings, but it was also anxious to ensure Germany's friendship in case of Soviet aggression. Thus a private organisation was set up to work under the German ambassador to recruit Finns for the SS. It was also agreed that, as far as possible, recruiting should be clandestine, and that the actual selection of volunteers should be handled by a Finnish committee with the help of an SS doctor. It was anticipated that 1,000 volunteers with previous military experi-

ence could be recruited in two months, and this was not to
include adventurers and idlers. In April the Finnish SS Committee
put forward three further conditions. Firstly, no Finnish volunteer
was to fight against England or Greece, in Africa, or against any
other state at war with Germany except the Soviet Union.
Secondly no Finn was to swear loyalty to Adolf Hitler, which
meant that a compromise had to be reached; it was agreed that
the oath would be to the Führer of the Greater Germanic Reich
(*Grossgermanischen Reiches*). Finally, in the event of another
Russo-Finnish war, in which Germany did not participate, the
volunteers were to be repatriated.

On 29 April 1941 the German ambassador in Helsinki was
informed that these additional terms had been agreed and would
be honoured as far as practicable and that recruiting could now
begin. By the end of May 1941, 1,251 Finns had been shipped to
Germany. This first draft included thirty-three Estonian veterans of
the Winter War, and most of the rest were of Finnic rather than
Swedish stock. This meant that the Finnish contingent was to
become the first SS unit to be composed of non-Germans and
non-Germanics.

Members of the Finnish Committee sailed to Germany with
the fifth and final draft on 5 June 1941. On arrival they were
alarmed to find that the first contingent, consisting of veterans of
the Winter War, had been attached to units of the *'Wiking'*
Division. They were somewhat mollified by the divisional
commander Felix Steiner's sympathetic attitude towards the Finns
and his assurance that once the Finns had learnt German tactics
they would join other contingents as an all-Finnish battalion. The
400 Finns in *'Wiking'* moved with the Division against the Soviet
Army on 22 June 1941 and fought well.

Meanwhile, the later drafts gathered at Wien-Schönbrunn
where they were formed into *SS-Freiwillingenbataillon 'Nordost'*
under a German commander. Almost immediately Berger began
to hear rumours that Finnish (and other foreign volunteers) were
complaining of inconsiderate treatment. The disproportionate
number of Finnish officers and NCOs meant that many of them
had not been given equivalent SS rank. As a corollary of this,
veteran Finnish NCOs were being treated like recruits by
inexperienced instructors, and this at a time when German
officers were being trained in the art of winter warfare by their
colleagues in Finland. To make matters worse, the *SS-Führungshauptamt* had released a number of superfluous Finnish
officers who returned home and criticised their treatment by the
SS. This did not augur well for future recruitment, especially as
the Finnish government had learnt of the situation and was
demanding the return of its citizens. A rapid improvement in the
lot of foreign volunteers in the SS meant that the Finnish Batallion
was permitted to continue.

From September 1941 the Finnish unit was known as the
Finnish Volunteer Battalion of the Waffen-SS (*Finnisches Freiwill-*

1 Collar patch worn by all
ranks. This is the
standard Waffen-SS
runic collar patch

2 Armshield of Finnish
manufacture which was
often worn by all ranks.
This particular example
belonged to a Swede,
Unterscharführer Axel
Ax. It measured
52mm×48mm (Svante I:
son Warfvinge Collec-
tion)

3 Armshield worn by all
ranks. This is the regulation German pattern and
measured 50mm ×
53mm (James van Fleet
Collection)

igen Bataillon der Waffen-SS). In February 1942 it was dispatched to the Mius front where it joined Division *'Wiking'* and became the third battalion of Regiment *'Nordland'*.

The Finns served on the southern flank of the eastern front in the Caucasus, on the Terek, at Hill 711 on the Mius, in the western Caucasus, in the oil-bearing area of Grossny, in the Kalmuck steppes and at Krasnoarmeysk. They fought well and as a result suffered heavy casualties which, to some extent, were made good by replacement personnel recruited by a new committee in Finland.

SS-Obersturmbannführer Hans Collani and his family. Collani, who was formerly in the *Leibstandarte-SS* 'Adolf Hitler' commanded the Volunteer Battalion *'Nordost'*, later known as the Finnish Volunteer Battalion throughout its existence

A Finn serving in Regiment *'Nordland'* wears the Finnish-made armshield and regimental cuff-band

By the end of 1942, as it became apparent to the Finns that Germany was not after all going to win the war, the Finnish government looked for an opportunity to conclude a separate peace with the Soviet Union. However, the existence of several hundred Finns in the Waffen-SS made it difficult to pursue a foreign policy independent of Germany. The Finnish government was having difficulties in replacing the heavy losses sustained on the eastern front, but Berger struggled and intrigued to keep the unit up to strength, even though many of the two-year engagements were about to expire.

At the beginning of June 1943 the Finnish SS men were sent home on leave, and the Finnish government then explained that it could not continue to provide replacement personnel for the Battalion. Moreover, Marshal Mannerheim himself made it quite clear that he did not wish volunteers to re-enlist. Rather than employ a force of considerably less strength than a battalion, the German authorities decided to put the best possible face on the matter. When the Finnish Battalion reassembled, its members were informed that their battalion had been disbanded. Its personnel were distributed among units of the Finnish Army.

While serving on the eastern front, 222 Finns were killed and 557 wounded. A few Finns continued in German uniform after the Finnish armistice of September 1944, but SS efforts to form a Finnish Volunteer Regiment met with no success, only five Finnish officers and 60 other ranks volunteering.

2 The Breton Nationalists

On 23 July 1941 Berger reported the existence of 400 Breton nationalists who had volunteered to fight against Communism on the eastern front. They did not wish, however, to serve alongside Frenchmen, and not even alongside French-speaking Belgians. Instead they had expressed their willingness to serve in the Flemish Legion, probably because they felt that the Flemings, being in a similar situation, would be sympathetic. The question of their enrolment was sufficiently important to be referred to Hitler. Although his decision is not known, it was probably negative for there is no record of any volunteers from Brittany in the ranks of the Flemish Legion.

3 The Ethnic-Germans from North Schleswig

In 1919 the German province of North Schleswig was returned to Denmark. The German minority had its own National Socialist Party *(NSDAP-Nordschleswig)*. Its members were disappointed when, on the capitulation of Denmark, Hitler decided not to annex the province as they had hoped.

Soon after the capitulation, a number of Danish subjects of German race volunteered to serve in the Wehrmacht and Waffen-SS. Himmler ordered that those who met the strict racial and physical standards of the SS were to be enrolled in the *SS-Totenkopf-Division*. If they met only German Army requirements they were to be sent to the 1st SS Infantry Brigade. Under no circumstances were ethnic-Germans to serve in the *Freikorps Danmark*.

In August 1942 the North Schleswig Nazi Party complained to Himmler that the parents of an ethnic-German volunteer killed on the eastern front had been informed that their son had died for 'the future of Denmark'. At the same time, another branch reported the desertion of a member of the community who had been obliged to serve in the *Freikorps Danmark* against his will. The following month the leader of the community *(Volksgruppe)* announced the death of three ethnic-Germans while serving with the *Freikorps*. On enquiry, Himmler ascertained that when the *Freikorps* received his order, it had been in action and consequently unable to post away its *Volksdeutsche*. Himmler again ordered that all ethnic-Germans serving in foreign legions were to be listed for redeployment.

4 SS Oaths

The oath for SS recruits

Ich schwöre Dir, Adolf Hitler, als Führer und Kanzler des Reiches Treue und Tapferkeit. Ich gelobe Dir und den von Dir bestimmten Vorgesetzten Gehorsam bis in den Tod, so wahr mit Gott helfe.

I swear to you, Adolf Hitler, as Leader and Chancellor of the Reich, loyalty and valour. I vow to you and all those you place over me obedience until death, so help me God.

The oath for Germanic volunteers in the Waffen-SS (circa 1940)

Ich schwöre Dir, Adolf Hitler, als germanischen Führer Treue und Tapferkeit. Ich gelobe etc.

I swear to you Adolf Hitler, as Germanic Leader, loyalty and valour. I vow etc.

The oath for European volunteers (circa 1941)

Ich schwöre Dir, Adolf Hitler, als Führer, Treue und Tapferkeit. Ich gelobe etc.

I swear to you Adolf Hitler, as Leader, loyalty and valour. I vow etc.

The oath for legionaries

Ich schwöre bei Gott diesen heiligen Eid dass ich im Kampf gegen den Bolschewismus dem Obersten Befehlshaber der deutschen Wehrmacht, Adolf Hitler, unbedingten Gehorsam leisten und als tapferer Soldat bereit sein will, jederzeit für diesen Eid mein leben einzusetzen.

I swear by God this holy oath that in the struggle against Bolshevism, I will unconditionally obey the Commander-in-Chief of the Armed Forces Adolf Hitler, and as a faithful soldier am ready, at any time he may desire, to lay down my life for this oath.

5 Legionary Commanders

SS-Freiwilligen-Standarte 'Nordwest'

3.4.1941 – 29.9.1941 SS-Standarten (1.9.41 Ober-) führer Otto Reich.

Freiwilligen-Legion Niederlande

7.1941 – 5.2.1943 *Luitenant-Generaal* H.A. Seyffardt was honorary commander (*Befehlshaber*) of the Legion until his assassination.

4.1941 – 7.1941	SS-Standarten (1.9.41 Ober-) führer Otto Reich. For a short time Reich was commander both of 'Nordwest' and the embryo Legion. Contrary to what has been written in most post-war publications, Luitenant-Kolonel G.W. Stroink was never officially appointed commander of the Legion.
7.1941 – 1.4.1942	SS-Obersturmbannführer Arved Theuermann (acting commander).
7.1942 – 20.5.1943	SS-Standartenführer Josef Fitzthum.

Freiwilligen-Legion Flandern

4.1941 – 7.1941	SS-Standartenführer Otto Reich.
7.1941 – 2.4.1942	SS-Sturmbannführer Michael Lippert.
2.4.1942 – 20.4.1942	SS-Hauptsturmführer Hallmann (acting commander).
20.4.1942 – 14.7.1942	SS-Sturmbannführer Hans Albert von Lettow-Vorbeck (named but never took up active command).
20.6.1942 – 15.11.1942	SS-Sturmbannführer Josef Fitzthum (acting commander).
14.7.1942 – 4.5.1943	SS-Hauptsturmführer Conrad Schellong.

Freikorps Danmark

19.7.1941 – 8.2.1942	Leg.-Obersturmbann (later SS-Brigade-) führer C. P. Kryssing.
1.3.1942 – 2.6.1942	SS-Sturmbann (later Obersturmbann-) führer Frederik Christian von Schalburg.
2 – 10.6.1942	Leg.-Hauptsturmführer Knud B. Martinsen (acting commander).
9 – 11.6.1942	SS-Sturmbannführer Hans Albert von Lettow-Vorbeck.
11.6.1942 – 6.5.1943	Leg.-Hauptsturmführer knud B. Martinsen.
2 – 6.5.1943	Leg.-Sturmbannführer P. Neergaard-Jacobsen (acting commander).

Freiwilligen-Legion Norwegen

1.8.1941	Leg.-Sturmbannführer Jørgen Bakke.
on 21.9.1941	Leg.-Sturmbannführer Kjelstrup (acting commander).
Autumn 1941 – 20.5.1943	Leg.-Sturmbann (later Obersturmbann-) führer Arthur Quist.

Finnisches-Freiwilligen-Bataillon der Waffen-SS

15.6.1941 – 10.7.1943	SS-Haupt (later Obersturmbann-) führer Hans Collani. Until 14 September 1941 Collani was commander of SS-Freiwilligen-Bataillon 'Nordost'.

Bibliography

Wartime publications

Auch Du. Herausgegeber der Reichsführer-SS, SS-Hauptamt, Ergänzungsamt der Waffen-SS, Wilhelm Lippert Druck-und Verlagshaus, Berlin.

Aufbruch: Briefe von Germanischen Freiwilligen der SS-Division 'Wiking'. Nibelungen-Verlag, Berlin 1943.

Dansk Daad Paa Ostfronten: Bogan om Frikorps 'Danmark'. Edited by Aage Nordahl Petersen, Trinitatistrykkeriet KBH, Copenhagen 1943.

Danske Helte: Breve fra Danske Frivillige paa Ostfronten. Det National Forlag, Copenhagen 1941.

Der Soldatenfreund, Taschenjahrbuch für die Wehrmacht mit Kalendarium für 1944. Ausgabe D: Waffen-SS. 24. Jahrgang Abgeschlossen mit dem 1 August 1943, Adolf Spornholz Verlag, Hannover 1943

Dich Ruft die SS. Reichsführer-SS (SS-Hauptamt), Verlag Hermann Hillger K.-G., Berlin Grunewald und Leipzig 1943.

Dienstalterlisten der Schutzstaffel der NSDAP. Personalabteilung des Reichsführers-SS 1934-44.

Frikorps Danmarks Kampe. Copenhagen 1944.

In 'T Verleden Ligt het Heden – Neerland's Grootheid in Beeld. Illustrated propaganda publication.

La Croisade de l'Europe contre le Bolshevisme. Illustrated French-language propaganda pamphlet, 1943(?).

Legionsminner- Trekk au den Norske Legions Histoire. Utgitt au Frontkjemperkontoret I Kommisjion hos Viking Forlag, Oslo 1943.

Mitteilungsblatt der Reichszeugmeisterei der NSDAP. Der Reichszeugmeister, Munich 1934-1945.

SCHAEPPI, Benno H.: *Germanische Freiwillige im Osten.* Buchverlag F. Willmy, Nuremberg 1943.

Sennheim-SS-Ausbildungslager. SS-Hauptamt Germanische Leitstelle, Strassburger Druckerei und Verlagsanstalt, Strasbourg.

SS-Befehls-Blatt. SS-Führungshauptamt, Berlin Wilmersdorf 1933-1941

SS für ein Grossgermanien. Assembled by Frits Reipert and published by Der Höhere SS-und Polizeiführer Nord, SS-Obergruppenführer und General der Polizei Rediess, Oslo 1942.

SS-Kameraden an allen Fronten. Der Reichsführer-SS, 1943.

Verordnungsblatt der Waffen-SS. Berlin Wilmersdorf 1940-1945.

Vlamingen op! 32-page illustrated Flemish-language recruiting pamphlet, Ergänzungsstelle Flandern der Waffen-SS, Antwerp 1942 (?).

Volg de Roepstem van eer en Geweten. Illustrated Dutch-language recruiting pamphlet, The Hague (?) autumn 1942 (?).

Post-war publications

ALKILS, N.: *Besaettelsestidens Fakta* (2 vols). Copenhagen 1945.

BAADE, F.: *Unsere Ehre Heisst Treue, Kriegstagebuch des Kommandostabes RF-SS.* Europa Verlag, Vienna 1965.

BENDER, Roger James and TAYLOR, Hugh Page: *Uniforms, Organisation and History of the Waffen-SS* (4 vols). R. James Bender Publishing, Mountain View California 1971-1975.

BRANDT, Willy: *Norwegens Freiheitskampf 1940-1945,* Auerdruck GmbH Hamburg 1948.

BROCKDORFF, Werner: *Kollaboration Oder Widerstand In Den Besetzten Ländern.* Verlag Welsermühl München,Wels 1968.

Denmark. *Betaenking (Beretning) til Folketinget afgivet af den Tinget under den 15 Juni 1945 Nedsalle Kommission i henhold til Grundlovens 45* (14 vols). Copenhagen 1945-1953.

HAAEST, Erik: *Frikorps Danmark-folk fortaeller* (3 vols), Bogan's forlag, Lynge 1975.

HEWINS, Ralph H.: *Quisling – Prophet without Honour.* W. H. Allen, London 1965.

IN'T VELD, NKCA: *De SS en Nederland* (with English supplement). Matinus Nijhoff, The Hague 1976.

JOKIPII, Mauno: *Pantti-Pataljoona – Suomalaisen SS-Pataljoonan historia.* Weilen & Göös, Helsinki 1968.

KLIETMANN, Dr K. G.: *Die Waffen-SS eine Dokumentation.* Verlag 'Der Freiwillige' GmbH, Osnabrück 1965.

KRÄTSCHMER, Ernst-Günther: *Die Ritterkreuzträger der Waffen-SS* (2nd edition). Plesse Verlag, Göttingen 1957.

KWIET, Konrad: *Reichskommissariat Niederlande: Versuch und Scheitern nationalsozialistischer Neuordnung.* Vierteljahshefte für Zeitgeschichte, 1968, No. 17.

LA COUR, Vilhelm: *Danmark under Besaetten* (3 Vols). Westermann Copenhagen 1946-1947.

LITTLEJOHN, David and DODKINS, Colonel C. M.: *Orders, Decorations, Medals and Badges of the Third Reich Vol. 2 including awards of German Volksgruppen, pro-Nazi Parties in occupied Europe, and the puppet states of Croatia and Slovakia.* R. James Bender Publishing, Mountain View California 1973.

LITTLEJOHN, David: *The Patriotic Traitors – A History of Collaboration in German-Occupied Europe 1940-1945.* Heinemann, London 1972.

MASON, Henry L.: *The Purge of the Dutch Quislings: Emergency Justice in the Netherlands.* Martinus Nijhoff, The Hague 1952.

MOLLO, Andrew: *Uniforms of the SS 1923-1945* (7 vols) Historical Research Unit, London 1968-1976.

Norges Krig 1940-1945, edited by Professor Sverre Steen (3 vols). Gyldendal Norsk Vorlag, 1947-1950.

TAYLOR, Hugh Page: *Uniforms of the SS Vol. 2 Germanische-SS 1940-1945* (2nd edition). Historical Research Unit, London 1970.

Rijksinstituut voor Oorlogsdocumentatie: *Het Proces Mussert*. The Hague 1948.

STEIN, George H.: *The Waffen-SS, Hitler's Elite Guard at War 1939-1945,* Cornell University Press, Ithaca, New York 1966.

STEINER, Felix: *Die Freiwillige – Idee und Opfergang*. Please Verlag Göttingen 1963.

STRASSNER, Peter: *Europäische Freiwillige – Die Geschichte der 5.SS-Panzer-Division 'Wiking'*. Munin Verlag GmbH, Osnabrück 1968.

VAN DER ZEEF, Sytze: *25,000 Landverraders- de SS in Nederland/Nederland in der SS*. Krusemann, Den Haag 1967.

TIEKE, Wilhelm: *Das Kaukasus und das Öl – Der Deutsche Russische Kampf in Kaukasien 1942-1943*. Munin Verlag GmbH, Osnabrück 1971.

TIEKE, Wilhelm: *Im Lufttransport an Brennpunkte der Ostfront*. Munin Verlag GmbH. Osnabrück 1971.

TIEKE, Wilhelm: *Tragodie um die Treue – Kampf und Untergang der III. (germ) SS-Panzer-Korps*. Munin Verlag GmbH Osnabrück 1968.

VAN HERP, Willy: *Wij vragen geen pardon*. De Clauwaert, Z.V.W. Leuven.

Vlamingen aan het Ostfront. Assembled by A. van Arendonck, Etnika ZVW Antwerp 1973.

Unpublished sources

ANAJA, Markus: *Germanska Frivilliga I Waffen-SS en kort oversikt*. Dissertation, University of Helsinki 1970.

ANAJA, Markus: *Tyskarna och de 'Germanska' Frivilliglegionerna*. Unpublished manuscript, Helsinki 1970.

BARTZETKO, Egon Alois: *Military Collaboration in the Germanic Countries 1940-1945*. Thesis, University of California 1966.

BUSS, Philip H.: *The non-Germans in the German Armed Forces 1939-1945*. Thesis, University of Kent at Canterbury 1974.

KNOEBEL, Edgar Erwin: *Racial Illusion and Military Necessity – A Study of SS Political and Manpower Objectives in Occupied Belgium*. Thesis, University of Colorado 1965.

Unpublished documents

Bundesarchiv 'BA' Folders NS 19 neu 27, 19 neu 1558.

Bundesarchiv-Militärarchiv in Freiburg. 'BAMÁ' Folder 64325.

Rijksinstituut voor Oorlogsdocumentatie, Amsterdam. Documents of the Befehlshaber der Waffen-SS in den Niederlande and of the Befehlshaber der Ordnungspolizei, Den Haag.

Legermuseum Leiden. Collection of wartime leaflets and newspaper cuttings, etc.

Foreign Office Library and Records Department London. 'FO' series 386, 855, 4641, 4647, 6509.

Royal Institute of International Affairs, Press Library, London. Newspaper cuttings collection.

Wiener Library, London. Newspaper cuttings collection.

Museet for Danmarks Frihedskamp, Copenhagen. Document collection.

National Archives of the United States of America, Washington. Microfilmed records of the Reichsführer-SS and Chef der deutschen Polizei T.175 Rolls 29, 67, 70, 106, 107, 109, 110, 111, 173, 174.

International Military Tribunal Nuremberg. Series RF.

US Military Tribunals Nuremberg. Series NG, NO, and NOKW.

Newspapers, magazines and journals

Berkenkruis – Maandblad van de Oud-Oostfrontstrijders, Antwerp 1953-1977.

Daggry—Tidsskrift for det Germanske Front – Og Kampfaelleskab 1944-1945.

Das Schwarze Korps – Zeitung der Schutzstaffeln der NSDAP organ der Reichsführung-SS, Franz Eher, Munich 1935-1945.

Der Freiwillige – Kameradschaftsblatt der Hilfsgemeinschaft der Soldaten der ehemaligen Waffen-SS, Munin Verlag GmbH, Osnabrück 1955-1977.

De SS Man – Kampblad voor Algemeene SS Vlanderen/Kampblad der SS in Vlaandern/Kampblad der Germaansche SS in Vlanderen, Antwerp 1940-1944.

Feldgrau – Mitteilungen einer Arbeitsgemeinschaft, Burgdorf/Hann. 1953-1966. Thereafter became *Zeitschrift für neuzeitliche Wehrgeschichte, Die Ordenssammlung,* Berlin 1967-1970.

Foedrelandet – For Danmarks Aere-Freihed- Og Ret, 1939-1945.

Germaneren – Kampforgan for Germanske SS Norge, Oslo 1941-1945.

Jul I Norden 1942. (Christmas issue of the DNSAP 'Aarsskrift') edited by A. Langaard Nielsen, DNSAP's Forlag Bovrup 1942.

Munin – Det Nye Norge I Bilder, Rikspropagandaledelsen 1942-1945.

Nordlandir, Viking Forlag A/S Oslo 1940-1945.

Storm SS – Blad der Nederlandsche SS-Weekblad der Germaansche SS in Nederland, Amsterdam/Groningen 1941-1945.

Wiking-Ruf – Zeitschrift der Hilfsgemeinschaft der Soldaten der ehenmaligen Waffen-SS, 1951 to March 1958 and thereafter combined with *Der Freiwillige*.

Articles

AALTONEN, B. S.: Das Finnische Freiwilligenbataillon der Waffen-SS. *Der Freiwillige,* 1957, No. 5.

Anon.: Das Finnische Freiwilligen-Bataillon der Waffen-SS. *Der Freiwillige,* 1966, Nos. 10 & 11.

Anon.: Die 23. SS-Panzer-Grenadier-Division 'Nederland' and Der Einsatz der Division 'Nederland'. *Der Freiwillige/Wiking-Ruf,* 1959, Nos. 3, 5 & 8.

Anon.: Der Schicksalsweg der norwegischen Freiwilligen-Division (sic) der Waffen-SS. *Der Freiwillige,* 1966, No. 4.

Anon.: Die finnische Jäger. *Deutsche Soldatenjahrbuch XIV* (Deutscher Soldatenkalender 1966), p.

Anon.: Mit dem Freikorps 'Danmark' zum ersten Einsatz. *Wiking-Ruf,* 1952, No. 4.

Anon.: Zur Kriegsgeschichte des Freikorps Danmark. *Der Freiwillige,* 1964, No. 9.

BERGER, Gottlob.: Zum Ausbau der Waffen-SS, Nation Europa, 1953, No. 4.

CARPINELLI, G.: The Flemish variant in Belgium Fascism. Wiener Library Bulletin Vol. XXVI (new series 1972-73 No. 28).

HAAPANIEMI, Kalevi: Ukrainassa ja Kaukasian vuorilla. *Yhyeishyvä,* September 1957.

HERZOG, Robert: Die Volksdeutschen in der Waffen-SS. *Studien des Instituts für Besatzungsfragen in Tübingen zu den Deutschen Besetzungen im 2. Weltkrieg,* 1955, No. 5.

HAYES, P. M.: Vidkun Quisling. *History Today,* 1966, No. 5.

JOKIPIII, Mauno: Suomalaisen SS-pataljoonan hajoittaminen v. 1943. *Historiallinen Aikakuaskirja,* 1960, Nr. II.

JOKIPII, Mauno: Suomalaista SS-patsljoona koskevista arkistolähteistä. *Eino Jutikkala.*

KAILA, Y. P. I.: Finnische Literatur zur Geschichte des Finnischen Frewilligen-Bataillons der Waffen-SS. *Feldgrau,* 1970, No. 2.

KLIETMANN, Dr K. G.: Die Deutsche Wehrmacht – Uniform und Ausrüstung 1934-1945 (Series I); No. 6 Die Freiwilligen-Legion Nederland der Waffen-SS 1941 bis 1943; and No. 19 Das Finnische Freiwilligen-Bataillon der Waffen-SS. *Die Ordenssammlung,* Berlin 1960.

KLIETMANN, Dr K. G.: Freiwilligen-Verbände im Kampf gegen den Bolshewismus. *Uniformen-Markt,* 1941, No. 15.

KWEIT, K.: Zur Geschichte der Mussert-Bewegung *Vierteljahreshefte für Zietgeschichte,* 1970, No. 2.

LOOCK, H. D.: Zeitgeschichte Norwegens. *Vierteljahreshefte für Zeitgeschichte,* 1965, No. 1.

LOOCK, H. D.: Zur grossgermanischen Politik des Dritten Reiches. *Vierteljahreshefte für Zeitgeschichte,* 1960, No. 1.

STEIN, George H. and KROSBY, H. P.: Das Finnische Freiwilligen Bataillon der Waffen-SS. Eine Studie zur SS Diplomatie und zur Ausländischen Freiwilligen Bewegung. *Vierteljahresheft für Zeitgeschichte,* 1966, No. 4.

STRASSNER, Peter: Das war 'het Legioen' von einsatz niederländischen Freiwilliger im Kampf gegen den Bolshewismus. *Deutsches Soldaten Jahrbuch XIV* (Deutscher Soldatenkalender 1966).

TIEKE, Wilhelm: Die deutsche Besetzung Dänemarks und Enstehung der ersten dänischen Freiwilligen-Verbände. *Der Freiwillige,* 1970, No. 7.

Picture Credits
Bogans Forlag 81 (left), 82 (top); Bundesarchiv facing 97, 123; B. L. Davis 134; Dodkins Collection 14; Historical Research Unit 4, 23, 25, 27, 28, 33 (top), 36, 38, 39, 40, 41, 51, 56, 71, 74 (top right), 75, 80, 83, 87, 88, 90, 91, 92, 93, 94, 95, 97, facing 121, 121, 122, 123 (top), 124, 125, 127 (bottom), 128, 132. Imperial War Museum facing 96, 110, 116, 117; Dr. Klietmann 122 (bottom); Musée Royal de l'Armée et d'Histoire Militaire 74 (top left), facing 81; Museet for Danmarks Frihedskamp 7; Brendt Nielsen 22, 77, 78, 79, 81 (right), 84, 85, 111; Private Collection 19, 24, 32, 33 (bottom), 34, 35, 44, 46, 47, 48, 49, 50, 55, 57, 60, 61, 62, 63, 64, 65, 66, 68, 69, 70, 72, 73, 74 (bottom), 96, 98, 99, 101, 102, 103, 104, 127 (top), 129; Rijksinstituut voor Oorlogsdocumentatie 3, 6, 20, 29, 52, 53, 58, 59 facing, 80, 121 (bottom left), facing 120, 126; L. Shaver 17; R. Smith 86 (top). Drawings of colours (between pages 120 and 121) by Malcolm McGregor and Pierre Turner.

Index